Also by Grace Firth · A Natural Year

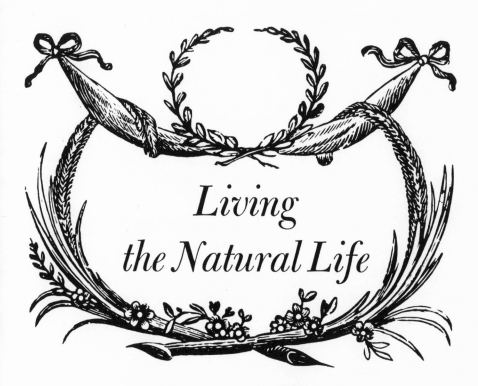

Living the Natural Life

GRACE FIRTH

Simon and Schuster · New York

SBN 671-21705-4
Library of Congress Catalog Card Number: 73-17620
Designed by Eve Metz
Manufactured in the United States of America

1   2   3   4   5   6   7   8   9   10

For Mother and Dad,
Lewis and Winifred J. Firth

Acknowledgments

I am deeply indebted to countless early-day documents that triggered my memory into times past. I am in the debt of my family who dauntlessly supported all of my trial and error adventures. I thank my family for their good natures (and stalwart constitutions).

I wish to express my special thanks to Nelle Haber, whose continued enthusiasm and editorial encouragement made this book possible.

Contents

1 · *Living the Natural Life*   9

2 · *Meat: Natural Means of Curing*   15

3 · *The Cure*   24

4 · *Some End Up in Sausage*   41

5 · *Go Native with Tea*   56

6 · *Fizzy Fun and Fortunate Coolers*   73

7 · *Pickle Power*   89

8 · *Just Naturally Potted*   106

9 · *Canned*   124

10 · *A Loaf of Bread, a Jug of Nuts and Fruit*   144

11 · *Safekeeping*   173

Bibliography   183

Index   185

1

Living the Natural Life

Living the natural life is more than gathering greens. Meat, drink, a tart bite, bread, sweets and, most importantly, saving nature's surplus, are vital parts to living the good life on Mother Earth.

I first came face to face with the fun of saving during "the year of the berry" in Seward, Alaska, where I was teaching Alaskan native children. I had circulated word that I would buy berries for a winemaking endeavor, not knowing that my expert berry-picker students would raid the hillsides and bring me over a hundred gallons of luscious fruit. Before long the tiny classroom burbled provocative odors that infiltrated the heating ducts and curious colleagues gathered for a closer sniff. Thanks to an understanding school cook (who later liberated two-thirds of my product), I moved my operation to a pantry and was again able to occupy my room without fear of drowning in fermenting berries.

That wine was great! Depth, body, clarity, zip all merged into a harmonious joy and hope. Preserving the gifts of the earth is a drink of joy; a pledge of faith in the future. As Schiller might have said,

> *Would he save mankind from ruin*
> *And aspire to God's own worth*

9

Living the Natural Life

Man must turn and pledge forever
Faith in ancient Mother Earth.

My second encounter with saving developed out of necessity.
I was lolling in the alders above the Kenai River experimenting
with a moose call, rubbing two sticks together, when crash,
wham! a bull the size of an overgrown mule sailed toward me.
I say sailed because all I could see were enormous antlers, knees
and wattles. I shot up through the wattles and had 730 pounds
of meat to preserve. Actually, packing-out that stone-heavy
moose rather shook my faith in the future—I doubted I would
have one. Later, after twenty-five trips between the alders and
the river, and a long night's sleep, I was ready to savor the joy
of saving. I sausaged, salted, pickled, jerked and embalmed
moose for posterity; that was good meat, too.

My penchant for saving originated with my frugal German-
Swiss grandparents with whom I lived as a child. They saved
everything: there were balls of string, tinfoil and beeswax, tins
of nail-type treasures, boxes of buttons, and every kind of preserved food. Grandma even saved the sludgy bottom of the wine
crocks, then ceremoniously poured the dregs down the kitchen
drain. She felt she was giving her bacterial best for the sewers
of St. Joseph, Missouri, where we lived. "Yeast is good for cess-
pools," she'd tell me.

After I met and married Lewis and we moved to the Virginia
suburbs of Washington, D.C., where he works in a government
office, I had my chance to practice living the natural life. We
bought fifty acres of hungry groundhogs and honeysuckle happiness near Boston, Virginia. The first summer Lewis and I and
the babies (ages 1, 2 and 3) tented there on the weekends, and
because our youngsters were not yet dry at night, and because
we had pitched our tent on a hillside, the five of us invariably
rolled off our pallets and awoke to find ourselves in a wet heap
near the door.

Building our cabin was Lewis's contribution to our being able
to live the natural life. With no electricity, and only a handsaw
and green pine, he hammered and the children handed him
nails while I hoed in the garden. Then, bone-tired, we'd go to
the river for a bath. Lewis and I would sit on a rock in the water and share a bottle of beer while the youngsters splashed, and
at dusk we'd all head for camp.

Every year our little wrinkle in the earth's surface changed a bit and we became more attuned to the pulse and needs of nature. First we planted trees in the washes. Next, thanks to a talented plumber, we acquired a real bathroom. Then we began a patio and learned about neighborliness. A man wandered into the clearing one day saying he had heard that we were working with stone and had "stopped by to help."

Lewis built on a lodge room with a loft for the children's delight, and a magnificent fireplace was created by a mountain artist who didn't hold with book learning but who left the world beautiful messages in stone.

The barn came next, then the pasture and the tractor. My garden grew, and before I realized what was happening, I found myself canning, drying, and preserving in ways half-remembered from my childhood.

After a nonprofit encounter with two skittish heifers, Lewis and I accepted our full co-heirdom to living the natural life the afternoon we got carried away at a livestock sale and bid on four calves. Before the day we eviscerated our bank account at the farmer's market, meat (for me) meant a chunk of ham oozing red-brown juices, steak, sausages, lamb chops, and hearty hamburgers, but after we bought stock, ownership with all its prides and agonies descended upon us. Home-raised meat meant utilizing and preserving all cuts.

My meat-preserving memories began with brisk November hog-killing days in Missouri. Next came dressing-out deer and skinning moose that had failed to outrun the train in Alaska. I remember squares of smoked game, wild moosewursts, beaver bacon, bearburgers and venison salami. Still, the idea of processing and preserving our own table meat was a confrontation.

Who was it who said, "With faith all things are possible"? I would amend that to read, "With faith, a willing husband and three eager children all things . . . ." The biggest boon in raising and preserving your own meat is the fun of it all.

Curing meat in the home adds a personalized dimension to contemporary living. It is a way in which families can touch base with a natural life. An Army sergeant we know buys meat by the half-carcass and after freezing part, he brines, dries, smokes and grinds out sausages. When his family of eight sits down to the table, they understand in a very real way that Daddy provides. They kid about his pickled jowl and jerked rump. Some measure the salinity of his brine and argue weight versus time in cure. Sarge proclaims to all that home-curing meat graphically fulfills the needs of a provider. He says that he gets response from his family through his mistakes as well as his successes and he receives recognition as the "Sausage Sarge" among his co-workers because "Everybody likes to talk sausage."

Home-brewed teas, soft beers and summer coolers lend down-to-earth rhythm and spice to the natural life. Lewis did not come from a true brew family as I did (my grandfather "brewed a bite from any fruit with fever"). But my husband did not hesitate, he jumped in with both feet. He once made a persimmon light beer that was so powerful he had to wear a crash helmet, goggles, leather jacket and gloves while evicting it from the bottles. The only thing soft about Lew's Persimmon Happiness was the peck of mashed persimmons and soft boiled sweet potatoes that he put into the crock.

Mild brews based on sugar or honey and flavored with herbs from the hedgerows have been popular since the lamps were lit before every tenth door in London. The brewing of ginger and spruce beers, meads and light ales are light-hearted chores even in the hustle and hop of today's life.

Peppery soft drinks are like peppery people: unpredictable. Sometimes they are hot tempered and should be put into a cooler before being confronted; sometimes they fizz into a reckless defiance; but more often they contain a satisfying secret ferment that embodies the meaning of life.

Regardless of the mature characteristics of homemade fizzy drinks, they should be handled with caution during their adolescence. Ever since my new sarsaparilla shot out the basement light, we restrict our youthful bottled beverages until they outgrow their temper tantrums. When well schooled we present them to society, and most soft beers develop into zesty, satisfying drinks.

Recently tea has been lumped into a single stereotype, "Tea," but for years Americans steeped tea from a variety of native herbs; they were natural teas, teas that had roots in the soil and reflected the land where they grew. They were identifiable both on the bush and in the cup. Native teas gave roots to the natural life: they were picked and dried according to the seasons and they gave a sense of fidelity to the future. The forager was reasonably sure he could return in years to come and pick herbs for tea.

An identifiable future is one of the gifts of living the natural life. Without faith in the future there is a tendency to live in the present, and often an ill-defined self evolves. Collecting and brewing natural tea combats rootlessness. Linden, Labrador, blossom, Blue Mountain or persimmon, all greet the senses with aromatic odors and clean flavors. Mints provoke pleasure in tall drinks. Tea is more than a tiny bag of brown crumbles. Native tea belongs to the earth, and preserving foraged tea preserves the underlying order of life.

Pickling is not my strong suit. But like my sourdough friend Patrick O'Petersen, who met every ship that docked in Seward for forty years in hopes that his "sweetheart" would descend the plank, I have kept my eye out for *the* pickle.

I have discovered that pickles have interesting things to say; some are queens of impudence, haughty and impatient sours; some are friends that blend with every occasion; and others are scoundrels, and burp bitter messages.

Lewis' home town in southern New Jersey was surrounded by acres of tomatoes, so his pickle communication leans toward catsups. I understand that they say marvelous things to each other, but I think that his catsups are jealous of me. When I try to make catsup it just lies in the pot waiting for a chance to burn and show up my negligence. Catsup and I do not get along.

Pickling, the preserving of fruits and vegetables in acid, is a natural way in which to create ambrosian flavors while deterring spoilage. Pickling early each fall puts you in step with the natural life.

Pot, potted, potting: ambivalent words in today's world. Authorities state that when ambivalence is present, noncommittal behavior is the result. Law, Church and school seem to suffer from ambivalence—positive and negative signs cluster simultaneously. Because of uncertainties, many people turn to nature for stability. The natural life breathes hope, they say, living in harmony with the earth eradicates ambivalence. Potting—the saving of surplus food by processing it, then spicing, salting and sealing it into earthen pots—does not usually result in uncertainty. Cheese, cooked meat and salted vegetables take on strong personalities when sealed in pots.

We started canning the year we planted seventy-five cabbages at our country cabin and each one ballooned into a trophy head. After loading our bounty into the back seat of the car along with our three youngsters, we herded our flock down the road toward home. A thundershower caught us, during which we had a flat tire and had to unload cabbages to find the spare. Next, one freaky worm frightened the girls and they screamed their terror for miles. Then an oncoming car in the wrong lane forced us into a ditch and cabbages poured into the front seat. But undaunted in spite of all this, we swung into our driveway determined to kraut and can our harvest. Canning, we discovered, is a carefree way to preserve vegetables and fruit together with year-long memories of the natural life.

Each winter as we eat our canned goods we relive the cycle of gardening and gathering: we feel again the urgencies of planting, we smell the earth as it opens its pores to the warm rain, we see again the waxy luster of ripening fruit, and we try to remember to thank God for His good world.

Breadmaking has long been my forte. There is nothing like a wad of dough to make a woman feel really wanted. Warm yeast smells from the kitchen, a hot, crisp loaf and crunchy-heeled dark breads smothered in jam add status to a woman's worth.

Someone once wrote that light bread, like a kiss, means ecstasy for youth, fidelity for the middle-aged, and homage for the old, but my grandmother said that light bread was the best-trod path to a man's heart. To me, homemade bread is great good food.

Sweets are timeless; natural sweets are moderators of harshness, uplifters of the spirit and a source of manipulative power. Nearly everyone has used sweets as a lever to induce another to carry out his wishes. I knew a honey-tongued man who brought my friend gumdrops, then sweet-talked her into converting six thousand dollars into cash and sailing to Mazatlan (in her boat), where he sent her ashore for sweet melons and left her on the beach.

Most sweet stories do not end in tragedy. Lewis courted me in Alaska with sweet wild strawberries. Later we discovered that rearing our offspring was filled with sweet pursuits.

Sweets, whether nibbles, dried fruit, youngsters, honey cake or a husband, add a sparkle of pleasure to living and preserving the natural life.

Meat:
Natural Means of
Curing

Our dreams of raising and eating our own meat began when Lewis and I cleared five acres of pasture at our cabin near Boston, Virginia. We had had fifteen acres fenced the previous summer but could hire no one to cut the pine for pulp. So, in February, armed with chain saw, tractor and eager spirits, we limbed and piled scrub greenery for latter-day bonfires. By June our newly seeded pasture was dense enough to support two calves and we went to market.

Our first error was buying heifers (Lewis has always been partial to girls); we learned later that steer calves generally gain weight faster than girly types. But as some sage said, "Sweet meat must have sour sauce," so we jumped into the sweet meat of the cattle business with two sorry heifers.

Sour-natured and scared, our livestock were only passing shadows until the dead of the following winter when they emerged from the pine and honeysuckle end of the pasture and started eating the dormant grass.

We made $7.50 on those wild, brush-clearing bovines and Lewis immediately plunged the profit into four calves. We thought they were steers, but one blossomed into heiferhood with a small hernia. We bought our calves in May and pastured them over the summer. Lewis built a corral. Then, on a snappy bright day full of autumn fragrance, we gathered nineteen of our neighbors for the roundup. Lewis' plan was to take three beef to market for sale, then truck the beautiful black Rumpelstiltskin to the slaughterhouse for table meat.

Great planning, but it contained one weak link: we couldn't catch the animals. The truck was in place, the herders were in top shape, but the cattle scattered, balled into a milling group, walked evasively away, waited for us to puff up behind them, then scattered again. Slippery and smart, our four calves toyed with us until it was too late to make the livestock market.

The next Saturday Lewis was determined not to be defeated. Up at the crack of dawn, with me as chief herder, he lured the cattle into the pen with sorghum-sweetened mash. This week one was missing. Alternating sweet cow calls with choice epithets, we scouted the pasture. Buzzards and crows soared with questioning circles, a fickle wind dropped and lifted the birds. We had not had breakfast, so my knees were rubbery and Lewis' nerves were frayed when our good-hearted steer finally appeared and trotted benevolently into the corral.

As we paused by the fence to say goodbye to our cattle I felt Mata Harian pangs in the pit of my stomach—we were selling our trusted friends into a feeder-lot existence. Calves weighing about 800 pounds are usually bought by commercial buyers who ship them to huge feeder lots where the animals are scientifically fed to gain two-plus pounds a day. (Our pasture-fed stock gained between one and two pounds a day.) With the exception of my hunger, I believe my biggest pang of the day was for dear Rumpelstiltskin, the small beef we were having butchered for our table. Faithful to the last, he dutifully munched mash. My concern was not related to the prospect of his slaughter. I worried whether or not he would be given adequate rations before the end. Rumpel loved to eat.

Later, when Lewis and I walked down the hill for breakfast, the pasture looked lonesome. We knew that within a few hours the truck would haul our stock to the sale and slaughterhouse, but even before the animals were gone, somehow the pasture looked empty.

No mother awaits the presentation of her debutante daughter more anxiously than a cattle seller waits for his calf to come through the auction ring. Will the good appearance, poise, alert eye, trim ankle be appreciated? Will the buyers note quality? Tiny twinges of "Will my baby get a good home?" sneaked into my thinking as I silently urged our calves to put their best hoof forward.

Marching resolutely into the arena, one of our steers faced Lewis and me eyeball to eyeball. No pleading, no remonstrance, no expression of discomfort or anguish was in evidence, but we wondered if our calf recognized us in the sea of faces that floated above him.

The bidding started, the ring manager noted our calf's good characteristics, the auctioneer's helpers hollered "Hup!" with vigor and pointed when the bid was raised. Our stock circled in the sawdust, figures flew, "Hear-a-quarter, hear-a-quarter, hear a quart, half, half, half, gotta quart, hear a half? Seventy-five, seventy-five!" The auctioneer jumped on the raise. "Hup! Hup!" Like the staccato chant and rhythm of an Indian dance, the auction jerked forward. Lewis and I sat, hardly breathing for fear we'd stop the action. "All around—all done?" The auctioneer signaled for the next lot of cattle to be brought into the ring while our noble animals retreated through a second gate. There was no backward glance.

Stretching my neck, I tried to see who had bought our beef. I played with the thought of approaching the buyer and telling him tidbits of information about his purchase, but the sale crier was singing out a new batch of figures and I was curious to see what other beef would bring.

At home that evening the pasture was even more empty, more lonely; I did not look at the corral. Lewis had made arrangements for Rumpelstiltskin at the slaughterhouse and I purposefully questioned him about the time required for hanging the meat, what cuts he had ordered and when we would pick up the frozen and packaged beef. For in my mind our stock was gone; in two weeks we would have a freezer full of beef.

Ritual is a mechanism by which the doors of life are opened or closed. I have heard of people "not able to swallow a bite of Old George" or whoever, but to our family the act of taking our stock to a sale or slaughterhouse closes the door. Another door opens when we utilize the meat. Whether it is named Flossy's ham or Rumpel's brisket, whether we eat the meat fresh, frozen or cured, table meat is divorced in our minds from the living animal. Surely no food was ever finer than Rumpel or Flossie or Toodles or George, or the old white ox from the highlands of Alaska; all were elegant on the hoof and on the plate.

Instant possession of two to four hundred pounds of lean muscle, fat and bone (plus a few other parts) overwhelms most iceboxes and families. Enzymes, bacteria and oxygen soon begin to taint meat, so the meat must be cooked (canned), frozen or cured to preserve it.

Curing meat is accomplished by permeating it with salt, saltpeter, sugar, spices, vinegar, spirits, by smoking, or by drying. Salt is the main ingredient.

Our ordinary mineral condiment salt (sodium chloride) at one time was considered so valuable by Indians in Alaska that it was used as a unit of exchange for women. A woman's worth was measured by her weight in salt; a squaw worth half her weight was considered to be shiftless, ugly or mean. Interior tribes fattened their daughters so that they would not bring shame on their families.

Although wives are not traded for salt today, meat and hides are still preserved in much the same manner as they were in the early days.

Meat bacteria which cause meat spoilage need moisture, food and warmth in order to grow. Salt draws moisture from meat; thus salt inhibits the growth of bacteria, but too much salt hardens food. Recipes vary, but rule-of-thumb for straight salt cure used to preserve meat is about twenty-six tablespoons of salt for ten pounds of meat. Sausage to be cured requires less salt, about ten tablespoons of salt to ten pounds of meat.

Saltpeter (potassium nitrate) also helps to reduce bacterial activity in meat and gives an attractive red color to cured meat. Saltpeter has toughening tendencies also, and like other "toughs" it must be handled with caution. I have heard warnings concerning harmful effects from ingesting saltpeter, but I have read no public statements regarding the use of saltpeter in meat cures. Again, recipes vary, but rule-of-thumb for use of saltpeter in curing meat calls for one scant teaspoon saltpeter per ten pounds meat for both straight salt cure and for cured sausages.

Sugar is added to meat cures to flavor and to soften the harshness of salt. (Rule-of-thumb calls for six-and-a-half tablespoons per ten pounds of meat to be salt cured.) My proclivity for burning foods is particularly active when cooking home-cured meats because they contain real sugar and they tend to brown more readily than commercially cured products. For that reason, I try to cook home-cured meats very slowly and, if possible, with moist heat.

Beer, wine and brandy, as well as vinegar, are sometimes added to meat-curing recipes as bad-bacteria inhibiting agents and as moisture and flavoring ingredients. Spirits are natural preservatives; a drop or two preserves harmony and harmonious sausages are the greatest!

Smoke from hardwoods such as hickory, oak or apple slows down the oxidation of fat and the growth of bacteria on surface meat. Smoke dries and adds a healthy glow with a woodsy bouquet.

The most popular home-curing methods are rubbing dry salt into the meat; rubbing a dry cure, a combination of salt, saltpeter and sugar, into the meat; or submersing the meat in a sweet pickle brine.

Time is essential because the curing ingredients must penetrate through fat and tissue as well as muscle. Bacon and smaller cuts cure faster than hams, so their time in cure is short, generally one-and-a-half days to the pound. Hams and shoulders take as much as three days in cure per pound of meat. Ground meats to be used in sausage are mixed with the cure ingredients so their time in cure is very short.

Meats may be pumped with a liquid curing mixture to speed up the curing action, but as a rule, time is the curer's best friend.

Country-style or home-cured meat usually means the use of dry cure or a sweet pickle brine. Both the dry and brine are applied to the outside of the meat and are slow-acting, so the pieces should be repositioned from time to time to insure an even take. This is called overhauling the meat. While overhauling, the meat should be tested by inserting a pointed instrument into the heavy muscles. Withdraw the probe and smell the point. If it has a clean, wholesome odor, the meat is curing properly; if taint has started, remove the meat from the curing vat, boneout or cut open, and rub the interior with fresh curing mixture.

One fall Granddaddy unknowingly dropped his paycheck into the curing barrel when overhauling the hams. He accused Grandma of washing his paycheck with his fireman's uniform. I still have the necklace he bought her when he found his brined check.

I heard of a man dropping a diamond ring into brine. He died, his widow found it and also found out about his girlfriend, who owned the ring.

Curing kegs can catch all kinds of things, so should be kept well covered.

After the time in cure is up, hams, bacons and other meats are simply soaked briefly, washed in lukewarm water, and hung to dry.   .

To discourage insects and to inhibit excessive drying, thoroughly dried meat should be wrapped in unbleached muslin, then in a layer or two of brown paper and stored in a large grocery sack. Do not hang cured products by a string that touches the meat because today's educated insects may use the string as a superhighway to their dinner. Missouri curers used to paint their meat storage sacks with a mixture of equal parts red clay, lime and flour moistened with water. Red sack meat, it was called. There was also a local beverage named Red Sack, so called because moonshiners often used the smokehouse as a base of operations and sometimes hid their product in meat sacks.

Insects, such as skipper flies, do not invade meat if the storage temperature is in the forties; my grandfather told me that cured meat does not develop a mature flavor if held at less than 40° F., so meat storage temperatures should be held between 40° and 50° F., if possible.

Utensils for curing meat are minimal: a lidded keg, crock or plastic trash can; a weight to hold the meat down; a pointed knife for testing; paper for wrapping; muslin; twine; and a clean secure storage area are the main requirements.

If you wish to make fermented, semi-dried or dried sausage, chopper power is the primary need. My husband and I go the "chicken" route. We ask the butcher to twice chop our trimmings so that they come out looking like red and white spaghetti. We mix our chopped meat with dry cure, flavor it with spices and spirits, then case it, hang it to dry, and seal each sausage.

The means of curing-your-own-sausage are as varied as the ethnic backgrounds from which sausages come. Generally speaking, the hotter the homeland of the ethnic sausages, the more efficient the methods of cure have been. Sausages of Italian background possess a lively personality, a robust spiciness and a keen, dry taste. Sausages of northern lineage are often semi-dry, droll, mild-mannered, easygoing and best when slightly fermented.

If pork is to be used in sausages that may be eaten uncooked, it is vitally important to pre-freeze the pork at minus-10° F. for twenty-one days. Prolonged deep freezing kills the trichinae sometimes found in pork which can infect man. The danger of trichinosis may be avoided by cooking pork thoroughly, but of course, this cannot be done if you plan to make ready-to-eat type sausages.

After the curing spices have been mixed into the ground meat, the meat is stuffed into casings. I make our casings out of unbleached muslin and Lewis made a stuffer out of a gallon-size plastic milk carton. In working with sausage all utensils should be sterilized by rinsing in boiling water. We boil our cloth casings.

Usually stuffed sausages should be cured for a few days at temperatures of around 55° F. in order to ferment or begin bacterial action. Later they are hung to dry in a cooler, bug-free area for a longer time. The last step in make-your-own salami is to seal each sausage with paraffin and wrap it in brown paper. Dried sausage should be stored in an airy, dark, predator-proof place, and refrigerated once it is cut.

If desired, some sausages may be smoked after they have completed their cure, but before sealing and storage. There are two main types of smoke: hot and cold. Cold smoke calls for a light smudge in a smoking chamber with heat of about 90° F. Hot smoke usually means a denser smoke with heat ranging from 120° to 170° F.

Cold smokehouses need not be elaborate. I have used old crates, an unoccupied dynamiter's shack and a dilapidated tee-pee. Some contemporary meat-smoking families utilize their covered metal charcoal grills as smokers. They hang the meat on one side of the grill and build a small smudge on the other side; the draft is left open and smoke circles the meat and the neighborhood, causing a flood of salivating friends to drop by. I followed my nose to such a smoker and was rewarded by scrumptious, soft, jerky-flavored beef. Neat electric smoking units may be purchased at leisure-time outfitters. These small metal smokers operate by igniting sawdust heaped on a hot plate; the meat is hung above the smoke and the temperature may be regulated by thermal control.

No matter which cold smoking apparatus is used, the hanging pieces of meat should not touch. Metal rods or wire should be stretched near the air vents at the top of the chamber so that the smoke will pass over the meat before filtering out. Plastic line should not be used.

Hot smokehouses are usually permanent, mouse-proof buildings with a door that locks. Years ago smokehouse thieves were as common as shoplifters are today. My grandfather knew a man who shot his wife full of salt pellets when he mistook her for a smokehouse thief. She never forgave him.

Hot smoke works on the same principle as that of cold smoke: the smoke and air filter around the meat and emerge through vents at the top. With temperatures of 120° F. and higher, the smoke partially cooks and dries the meat but time in hot smoke is usually shorter than the time required for cold smoke. Permanent smokehouses are built with a stone floor on which a small smudge is kindled and the meat is hoisted away from the heat or lowered to adjust temperatures.

Temperatures in a smokehouse should be raised gradually; if heat is raised too high too fast, shrinkage and shriveling will occur. Sausage will pop. If you have ever circled your smoke chamber scooping up popped sausage, you'll heed the mother's admonition to her airman son when she cautioned him to fly "low and slow."

When cured meat or cured sausages have completed their time in smoke, they should be handled as plain cured products. Meat should be wrapped in muslin and paper and hung in a dry, clean, cool, well-ventilated area, and sausage should be sealed by dipping in paraffin or lard and wrapped in paper before storing.

Lewis made a screen storage box out of aluminum screens that we bought from a junk dealer. The box is splendid, large enough so that the meats can hang freely, but small enough to be moved.

One caution: do not store meat near fuel oil. I remember ten thousand dried and smoked salmon at Eklutna, Alaska, that were flavored with petroleum. Throughout the winter everyone burped kerosene and the furnace man joked about the hazards of his job.

Smaller cuts of meat should be eaten before the larger pieces because they tend to lose quality earlier. Sausage may be eaten as soon as it tastes good, but it is traditional to wait until spring holy days to cut a ham.

Our family has always felt virtuous about being able to wait until spring to cook a ham but I recently talked with a lady who stated that she held her hams at least five years before eating them. She added that a six-month-old ham is like an infant just developing character. I was ashamed to tell her, but our infant hams possess personalities, and I know quite a few babies with definite characters at six months, too. But the beauty of curing your own meat is that it can be eaten at any time.

Whether you raise your own or buy it by the hoof or half, whether you cure meat with salt, spices, spirits or smoke, whether you put down big hunks or make up squiggly sausages, meat curing is a joy. Preserving meat in the home illuminates the underlying order and meaning of living the natural life.

3

The Cure

I grew up brining and smoking. My grandparents, with whom I lived, usually butchered a hog each November. As a child in Missouri, I sometimes felt ashamed of the home-cured meat in my school lunch sandwiches, and I eyed my schoolmates' store-bought luncheon meat enviously. But times have changed. The hearty, home-cured meat that embarrassed me in my youth is welcome in our suburban home. Today my husband, Lewis, and our three young people, Martin, Marie and Penny, delight in sinking their choppers into our home-cured hams and bacon.

We do not raise our own porkers nor do we butcher, but we enjoy putting down the meat.

When pork prices and our freezer meat level are low we make reservations at a legitimate slaughterhouse, not for ourselves but for a pig. Inspected houses are recommended. Butcher-by-night operators usually have no government inspector on the premises as required by law, and you may or may not get your meat. Murky's place, down past the sawmill, across the tracks, behind the third shack on the right, was busted last December and seven carcasses of "nobody's" meat were destroyed. I heard of another illicit slaughter man who absconded one night with the fifteen porkers he had contracted to butcher. "What pigs?" he asked when he was approached the following day.

After securing a berth for our prospective pig, Lewis and I go to a livestock auction market, pick out several likely-looking porkers in the two-hundred-and-fifty-pound range, then bid when our choice marches through the ring.

Next, we make arrangements with a trucker to transport our prize to the slaughterhouse.

Fourth, we follow the pig to the meat plant and write our order for the meat: so many chops to a package, roast sizes desired and the number of pounds of fresh sausage that we want.

The pig is killed, dressed, cut, wrapped and frozen; ready for us to pick up in a week.

Bidding on your own pig can be fun, but filled with shaky situations, too. (Sitting high up, I am always scared of falling into the arena and being trampled underhoof, or worse, auctioned off.) One autumn Lewis and I picked out a long, lean white pig in the pen and when it came through the ring, we bid. Somehow our bid was missed. Cross and crestfallen, we substituted a roly-poly red one, but we left the auction harboring bitterness because we had missed our first choice.

When the trucker came by to be paid for delivering our pig to the slaughterhouse, he asked if we had heard the news: the white hog had dropped dead after it had been purchased.

"Who paid for it?" Lewis asked. The trucker shrugged his shoulders and said, "In the livestock business, it's buyer beware."

Other "beware" areas surround the novice. One danger area is the cost factor. A neighbor bid on a vealer by its mother's side and when he went to the office to settle up, he found he had bought the cow, too. He had interpreted the auctioneer's figure price as "by the head," which is the way vealers are sometimes sold. To his shock, he found that he had been bidding on both animals "by the pound." "Thirty cents a pound for old cow meat makes pretty expensive hamburger," he lamented. Rule-of-thumb: you double the price of meat on the hoof when calculating the cost of butchered, hung, cut, wrapped, ground and frozen meat.

Beware of unknown truckers hired to transport your animal to the slaughterhouse. Another neighbor told me that he had purchased a prime Duroc Jersey hog at 235 pounds, and a toothless black sow weighing 350 pounds was delivered. Careless truckers can bruise the meat, or harm the animals in other ways such as overcrowding, holding them with no water, or allowing them to become unduly excited. To be safe, go along with your porker to its destination.

The value of an efficiently run slaughterhouse is reflected in the quality of meat you receive. Cleanliness at every stage is imperative. Proper chilling of the carcass is important. The animal to be butchered should be handled in a quiet manner; excitement before slaughter taints the meat.

A reputable slaughterhouse will invite prospective customers to inspect their premises. Beware of slaughterhouses that are dirty, that have messy pens with flies and rodents, and those that have small cooling or chilling facilities. Ask other customers if they have ever suspected missing meat. In some places it is common practice for slaughterhouse workers to "lift" as much as 20 percent from a carcass. They either sell it on the sly or eat it themselves.

Ordinarily a pig will yield a carcass weight of about 75 to 80 percent of its live weight. A 250-pound hog will dress out to between 185 and 200 pounds of meat, trimmings and fat. About 60 percent of the dressed weight will be ham, bacon, shoulder and loin. Sausage trimming, ribs, neckbones and head will average around 20 percent of the dressed carcass; fat and other parts will make up the remaining 20 percent.

When you do not take the fat or the head and receive your meat cut, frozen and neatly packaged, "lifting" is difficult to perceive. I read an 1855 account of a police official who caught meat "lifters" by painting several meat carcasses with "a searching cathartic," but this cannot always be managed successfully.

Short of infrared eyeballs, X-ray vision, or a brother-in-law who butchers, "know your meat cutter as you know your banker" seems to be good advice.

Bacons or sides of pork represent about 10 percent of the carcass, hams total 18 or 20 percent of the carcass weight, and shoulders or picnics account for about 15 percent of the dressed weight.

The curing of hams, shoulder meat and bacons is a relatively simple procedure. Although we have mixed our own dry cure (eight pounds salt, two pounds sugar and two ounces of saltpeter—to which some curers add a four-ounce can of black pepper—for every one hundred pounds of meat to be put down), we usually purchase the commercial, ready-mixed product. This is available at rural grocery stores or farm suppliers.

If you mix your own cure, a thorough blending is extremely important because the quantity of saltpeter is so small it may end up in one spot.

It is also important to weigh the individual meat pieces accurately. Too much salt makes the meat dry and hard; too little encourages spoilage.

To cure bacon and hams, keep the meat cold, as close to 38° F. as possible, but it should not be frozen. Weigh the meat and divide the total amount of dry cure required into two parts. Rub one part of the cure on all surfaces of the meat with a soft kneading motion, and poke some into the shank ends of the hams. Stuff it under the outer edges of the skin and pack it into every crevice and cranny. Pat a layer on the lean faces of the meat and spread some on the bacon strips. The heavier cuts should receive heavier amounts of dry cure. Fit the meat into a clean plastic trash can, crock or barrel (metal is not recommended) and sprinkle more dry cure over each layer as it is packed. Hams should be placed on the bottom, skin side down, and the lighter pieces layered on top, with the topmost bacon skin side up. Sprinkle a layer of dry cure mixture on top, weight the meat and cover the container.

Mark your calendar with the estimated day your meat is to be resalted with the remaining half of the curing mixture (about a week after the meat is put down); and mark the days on which your bacon and hams should be removed from the cure. Bacon usually takes one-and-one-half days to the pound, and hams should stay in cure two or three days to the pound. If the weather is warm, meat will cure a little faster than if it is cold. Do not let the curing meat freeze.

Haul the meat out of the barrel and resalt it with dry cure after about a week. Using the second half of the curing mix, rub each piece as before and repack the meat in a different position so that the cure will be uniform. Some people reposition the meat every week but add no more dry cure after the second application.

Give the cure plenty of time. If you plan to keep the meat over summer, give it a little extra time in cure. Test the larger pieces with a probe to see if they smell "clean," and if the cure is penetrating around the joints.

One of the most important factors in a good cure is temperature. The curing container should be kept between 38° and 40° F.

for best results. However, we cured hams one summer by suspending the plastic trash can in the spring where the water temperature remained 48° F. and they were fine.

There are many ways to cure hams. A soft-spoken neighbor from Georgia packs her fresh hams with the directed amount of commercial dry cure, then lays them on a thick pad of old newspaper in her cool basement. She says this allows them to bleed. Every day or two she pats on more cure and turns the hams. When the hams no longer show any sign of dripping, she turns them every day for one week. Then she mixes four ounces of ground allspice with four ounces of black pepper in the remaining sugar cure and adds a pint of syrup. "Sugar cane syrup," she explained, surprised that I did not understand just "syrup." She covers her hams with the spiced paste, wraps them completely in muslin, in brown paper, then in a second wrapping of brown paper, and finally slips each bulky package into a double grocery sack, and hangs them in a dark, cool place.

My friend ages her Georgia hams until July. After that, she scrubs off the moldy cure with hot water, soaks her sugar-cured ham overnight in cold water, simmers it for a whole day, and lets it cool in its own water before she bakes it. Baking is a brief glazing operation. Lastly, the ham is cooled and refrigerated.

According to my neighbor, cold Georgia ham, thinly sliced, served with heaping platters of hot crisp-fried chicken and eaten with friends in the back yard, is an All-American way to celebrate Independence Day.

Most dry-cured hams and shoulders should be scrubbed, soaked in cold water, and boiled or cooked with moist heat before baking.

Pickle-cured hams and bacon are essentially the same as dry-cured meat. The technique differs in that the fresh pork is submerged in a liquid or brine instead of being rubbed with dry salt cure. Pickle brine for one hundred pounds of meat is made by dissolving eight pounds of salt, two pounds of sugar and two ounces of saltpeter in four-and-a-half gallons of water. The meat is placed in a plastic trash can, weighted, and the pickle is poured over it. Pickled, or brined, pork must be overhauled and repacked in the same brine on the seventh, fourteenth and twenty-eighth days. Changing position gives a uniform cure and by positioning the meat carefully it may be properly shaped.

The Cure

Curing time for ham in pickle cure is four days to the pound, minimum twenty-eight days, and bacon needs two days to the pound, fifteen days minimum. Meat should be rinsed when taken from the pickle and hung to dry before wrapping or smoking.

If the pickle solution becomes spoiled, that is, sour-smelling and ropey, throw it away. Wash the meat and repack it in new pickle cure.

My grandfather sometimes submerged his hams and bacon in a pickle made of one gallon of water and one pint of wine vinegar into which he dissolved two pounds of salt, two cups of sugar and one tablespoon each of pepper, cloves, mace and saltpeter. He stirred the pickle and repacked the meat every few days for thirty days, then he rinsed each piece and hung it to dry for a week. Sometimes he smoked the pork with a cold smoke, three hours to the pound, but smoked or not, his pickled hams and bacons were flavored with a winey tang that was different. We often started eating the bacons right away, but Granddaddy wrapped and aged the hams.

Whether we use the dry-cure method of processing pork, or the sweet pickle brine, we soak our meat for thirty minutes in fresh water when the curing period is completed. Next we scrub each piece with a stiff brush, rinse and hang the meat to dry in a clean, cool place for about a week.

After the cured pork has dried, some people rub the meat with pepper, brown sugar and ground cloves which have been moistened with a little sherry. They then wrap the meat in several layers of cheesecloth and brown paper. Others poke borax around the ham bone and cover the meat with black pepper before wrapping it. We simply wrap the cured, rinsed and dried hams with muslin and two wrappings of brown paper and slip them into a grocery sack before we hang them. Wrapping is not absolutely necessary but it slows down excessive drying and oxidation of the fat and deters insect infiltration.

Some people smoke their cured and dried meat before they wrap it. Pork to be cold smoked is hung in the smoke chamber and a light smudge of hardwood smoke is allowed to filter around the meat. The temperature is held at approximately 90° F. We cold smoke our bacons for about a day, or until a glossy straw color develops, and the hams are held at 90° F. in a light smoke for three days. The temperature of the smoke should not be hot enough to draw grease because the ham will shrink and dry out.

One year in Alaska the Cooper River Indians kindled a hot smoke for their salmon, and the fish dripped. At school recess little boys crowded in the smokehouse and licked up the pungent grease with their fingers, then returned to school smelling like smoked salmon. The fish were overly dry that winter; they tasted like fishy wood chips.

Whether we smoke our cured pork or not, the wrapping and storing by hanging in a cool, dry place is the same. We usually eat the bacon shortly after it is cured, but we try to keep our hams until spring.

Country or home-cured bacon should be tasted on its own merits. If you think neat, standardized commercial bacon, you will be disappointed. Home-cured bacon is lusty both in flavor and slice size. I leave the rind on the slab and cut the meat away from it as we use it; a friend in Maryland takes her bacons and hams to the butcher for slicing.

Because real sugar is used in curing, country bacon burns readily in the skillet, so it should be fried slowly and turned often until crisp. Eggs cooked in home-cured bacon fat need little salt and they seem to explode their own special goodness into breakfast.

My teen-agers love a breakfast of diced, crisp fried bacon in cream gravy over toast. I fry a handful of diced bacon, pour off most of the grease, sprinkle the meat with two tablespoons of flour, mix, add two cups of milk, simmer and stir for two or three minutes, and pour over toast. I add applesauce to the menu and feel that all are adequately fueled to charge into their respective worlds.

Bacon on Country Pizza makes an excellent supper.

Preheat the oven to 450° F. Roll pizza dough (or a hunk of bread dough which has been saved in the icebox) thinly on a large greased cookie tin. Break one egg into a pint of sour cream, mix well with a fork and pour over the pizza dough. Spread the cream evenly, sprinkle with one large handful of raw diced bacon and one large handful of raw diced onion. Sprinkle a pinch of parsley on the pizza for color, add pepper and salt, and pop the pizza into the oven for twenty minutes. The sour cream will rise up and become cheesy, the onion will sink comfortably, and the bacon will cuddle up in its own juice.

The Cure

Whether you use home-cured bacon or the store kind, whether you create your taste bud treasure to entice a strange man or to feed a sweet husband, Country Pizza is Total Food.

The southern way to cook cured jowl is to simmer it with pre-soaked blackeyed peas. In our family a heaping bowlful of hog jowl and blackeyed peas before the game on New Year's Day goes over great.

Baked country ham, elegant for dinner, lasts and lasts for cocktail snacks, breakfasts, and many lunches. We usually finish off with ham hash and, finally, ham bone soup. Home-cured ham seems to retain its individuality longer than commercial hams and every ham is a little bit different. Someone once said that variety in life opens new windows and hope comes in. Our hams have not lacked variety; some have been salty slims, some nutty good-guys, and others jolly fat boys. I scrub, soak overnight, parboil, then bake our country ham. Sometimes I remove the bone after baking if it comes loose, then sew the meat into a cloth sack to shape it before putting it into the icebox. To savor its stouthearted flavor, we slice our cold ham very thin.

A man I know who says he is the official ham cook in his house roasts the washed and soaked ham thirty minutes per pound in a tightly covered pan to which he has added one bottle of port, nothing more.

Stuffed ham, southern Maryland style, is my husband's favorite. Philip H. Love, in his nationally syndicated column "Love on Life," wrote, "Fie on Wife Who Refuses to Make Stuffed Ham." He then gave his wife's recipe for stuffed ham.

Soak a country or home-cured ham in cold water overnight. Wash and parboil the ham for twenty minutes, remove the skin, let it cool, then cut three lengthwise slits down one side of the ham, then two slits across, then three down each side of the ham. (The reason for alternating the slits is to make sure that, when stuffed, one will not break into another.) Wash and drain one quart of Brussels sprouts, three pounds field cress, three pounds kale; and one-half stalk celery. Chop the greens into one-inch pieces, dice one small red hot pepper and mix. Tie all the greenery in a cheesecloth and drop into the boiling water from which the ham was removed. Blanch for three minutes, remove and drain. Cool and thoroughly mix in one teaspoon black pepper, one-quarter teaspoon red pepper, and two tablespoons of celery seed. Stuff the limp greens into the slits made in the ham. Fill the slits from both sides, pile the remaining greens on the top of the ham and place the ham skin side up on a large piece of cheesecloth. Draw the cloth tightly around the ham, folding it at the top, and sew the cloth securely. Return the stuffed ham to the same water and simmer for fifteen minutes per pound. Test with fork and when done, let the ham cool for two hours in the same water. Slice and serve when cool.

With baked sweet potatoes, a whipped green Jello-avocado salad and chocolate cake, stuffed ham is a completely scrumptious Easter Sunday dinner.

My grandmother used to cook ham in sweet hay. Instructing Granddaddy to bring home a bag of clean, fragrant hay, she'd soak a large home-cured ham overnight and the next day sew it into a muslin bag. Placing the ham boiler on the back of the cook stove, she would layer a bed of hay in the bottom, then the ham, and lastly stuff more hay around the meat. The boiler was filled with water, covered, and left to simmer overnight while provocative odors of rich meat and summer meadows danced through the house.

As Granddaddy carved the big brawny chunks of meat he would say that boiled ham served with little potatoes creamed with onions, stewed apples, and hunks of bread would make a saint out of any sinner.

In contrast to the warmth of pungently flavored home-cured ham, there is nothing more bleak than cold cuts of poorly cured beef. Corned beef is often shameful, stringy, prideless meat with yellow fat flopped to one side. A British friend tells me that good corned beef begins in the butcher shop, for a good butcher, like a skillful tailor, can "handle the material" and make it proud.

For proper corned beef, my English friend trims the brisket into uniform thickness, making sure that each piece is five or six pounds in weight. If she uses blade, she removes the bones. To brine each ten pounds of meat, mix three cups of salt, one cup brown sugar and three teaspoons saltpeter with one gallon of water and boil the pickle for fifteen minutes; then, skim it. When it cools, immerse the beef in it. Turn the beef every day, keep it well covered in brine for thirty days, then cook it or hold it in the same cure until needed. She says that some people rinse and dry their corned beef and wrap it as they do pork.

Before cooking home-cured corned beef, soak it in cold water for a couple of hours. Then bake it in a tightly lidded pan with about an inch of water in the bottom, at about 350° F. for three or four hours. With a tomato and lettuce salad and pear chutney this baked corned beef makes an excellent lunch.

When beef is kept in brine, it should be checked regularly because at temperatures above 38° F., it is likely to "rope," or the brine seems to thicken. If this is noticed, the beef must be removed, rinsed and repacked with new brine in a sterilized container.

For kosher-style corned beef, rub the brisket, plate, flank, or boneless chuck with chili powder. Make a spice liquid of one quart of water, one-and-a-half tablespoons of ground black pepper, three-fourths tablespoon of ground white pepper, two tablespoons of mixed pickling spice and a bay leaf. Simmer for one hour, strain, cool and add a teaspoon of either garlic or maple flavoring. Stir this spice liquid into two gallons of curing pickle (three-and-one-half pounds of commercial dry cure dissolved in two gallons of water) and immerse the meat in it.

After one week change the position of the corned beef and leave it in cure for a second week. The beef may then be cooked or held in the cure. If it is to be held, the cure should be diluted with a quart of boiled and cooled water and the holding temperature kept at about 40° F.

Before cooking, this corned beef should be rinsed and soaked for an hour in cold water. Then put an eight-pound piece into a deep oven pan, surround it with chopped apples and onions, spice it with pepper, bay leaves and garlic, dump in a water glass of red wine, and fill the pan with water. Cover tightly and slip it into a moderate oven for six hours.

When done, strain and rinse the apples and onions in warm water to get rid of excess grease, mash them with a cup or so of the corned beef juice, then spoon them like a gravy over the sliced hot corned beef. Kosher corned beef served with rice cooked with carrots and flavored with olive oil and a sprinkle of dried mint is straightforward good fare. I have also served this spicy kosher beef with goulashka—cooked noodles, butter and shredded cabbage steamed four minutes together and seasoned heavily with paprika.

Traditionally, in March our family requests corned beef, which we make by immersing brisket in brine (three-and-a-half pounds of commercial sugar cure to two gallons of water) and holding for two weeks. I rinse the beef and boil it in a big kettle of water until tender. About one hour before dinner I add a huge pan of whole, peeled potatoes; then five minutes before sitting down to the table I spoon out the spuds and drop in a head of chopped cabbage. I boil the cabbage with the meat for four minutes, drain and serve the corned beef, cabbage and potatoes separately. As one of my less delicate relatives says, from then on it's "slump and grunt."

One Christmas in Alaska a big-boned, tender-hearted teacher who lived on the Kenai Peninsula invited some of us to share her holiday ox. Actually I knew the old ox well and was glad to pay final tribute to him. Five-foot snowdrifts precluded our driving to her homestead, so we donned our skis, tied our gaily wrapped gifts to our backs, and skiied across the Homer Upland. Margaret Cutler's husband had the smoker going; wisps of sweet alder smoke climbed the brittle, cold air; and we could see and smell the hanging ox round as we came over the hill. When we peered through the smoke at close range we could see the tiny red-brown droplets of goodness blistering and bubbling from the ox meat, and we could not contain ourselves. Taking a knife, Margaret sliced off a nibble. Tough ambrosia! The fresh ox round had been rubbed daily for three weeks with black peppercorns, juniper, onions, salt, brown sugar, allspice and red wine; it had been smoked for thirty-six hours; and that evening Margaret put the spiced ox on a rack in a deep cast-iron cooker, layered it with strips of bacon, poured in a quart of port, covered the pot and roasted it on the back of the cook stove overnight.

The old white ox outdid himself. The next morning, when the other holiday guests began to arrive by plane, snowshoes and skis, we removed the lid and the spicy fragrance of that beautiful ox permeated the highlands for miles around. At noon the buffet table audibly groaned under its thirty-three-pound bounty of meat.

Served with homemade bread, a huge watercress salad that was flavored with shallots, hunks of king crab swizzled in clarified butter, dishes of razor clam dressing and sweet scalloped potatoes, the spiced ox was praised by all who tasted it and proclaimed the Prince of Meat. It was a glorious end to the noble animal that had pulled Margaret and me in a two-wheel ox cart on a seven-day trip around the Kenai. Spiced ox on Christmas Day was a grand way to pay homage to a beast that had been our friend. Old-timers in Homer still brighten at the memory of that gorgeous beef.

Years later, "Mother's Corned Rump" on a North Carolina dinner menu startled my husband and me. Of course, we had to try it and the meat was everything a corned rump should be. I stepped behind the counter to compliment the cook and learned that it was on the menu every Thursday. "I got salesmen that carry their wives one hundred miles just to let them stick a fork into my rump, so they tell me," the good-natured cook said without cracking a smile. "Got the recipe from my mother," she added.

For six pounds of meat, dissolve one-third cup salt and one teaspoon of saltpeter in water, add six peppercorns, a red pepper pod, six coriander seeds and four whole cloves. Simmer for twenty minutes and cool. Pour over the meat and add enough water to cover. Weight the meat and set it in a cool place for one week. On the morning the beef is to be cooked, pour off the liquid, rinse the meat, cover with water and simmer for two hours. Chill, slice three-eighths of an inch thick against the grain, place the slices on a platter, cover with foil, and put in the oven to rewarm.

Mother's Rump was served with "Soft Tomatoes," boiled rice flavored with saffron and delicious hush puppies.

I never mastered the hush puppies, but delicate soft tomatoes are delicious. Slip the skins from six firm tomatoes. In a skillet, over a low fire, melt one-quarter cup butter and stir in two teaspoons of tarragon leaves, one teaspoon lemon juice, and a sprinkle of white pepper. When well mixed, carefully lay the whole tomatoes in the skillet, salt and sugar them, and spoon some butter over each. Turn the tomatoes gently and cook for four minutes on each side, or until they weep. For a pretty dish, serve immediately because they will not hold; but plump or flat they certainly go with Mother's Corned Rump.

Tongue and tail, teat and tripe, all pickle into spiced tidbits. Although most steers come equipped with tongue and tail, you have to catch the butcher before he disposes of them or you miss out on the pickle happiness.

Corned ox tongue used to be my grandmother's hole card when her kin visited unexpectedly. One family must have thought we lived on tongue; every time their car wheezed to a stop in front of the house, Grandma put a tongue to soak.

To cure beef tongue, trim and wash, then prick the tongue all over with a large darning needle. Pricking a tongue is a satisfying task. As I poke, I mentally prick tongues that have hurt others—sometimes it is my own tongue that gets the business. The next torture is to rub salt (one cup that has been well mixed with a pinch of saltpeter) into the tongue. Lay the tongues in a plastic bucket for half a day while you boil and cool a brine made of a gallon-and-a-half of water, two cups of salt, two teaspoons of saltpeter, two cups of brown sugar, ten black peppercorns, a bay leaf and a teaspoon of marjoram leaves. Pour the cooled brine over the tongues, weight them and leave them in brine for one week.

The tongues may then be removed, rinsed and cooked, or they may be hung to dry before being wrapped for storage. Grandma used to soak the cured tongues for two hours in cold water, then boil them for two hours with a teaspoon of pickling spice. After the boiled tongues are well done, they should be momentarily dropped into cold water, peeled while hot, and sliced. Corned ox tongue has a delicate, all-beef flavor, and if sliced with discretion even the most picky eater will relish it. I eat beef tongue with horseradish and Lewis likes it sopped in catsup.

In addition to preserving beef by corning, some early Midwesterners dried beef. Alaskans of remote areas still dry surplus meat, using much the same technique that their forebears used. Venison, like beef, makes excellent dried meat or jerky, but dried moose suffers from delusions of grandeur and swells to enormous proportions when chewed. The longer you chew dried moose, the bigger it gets.

I have not dried beef, but I have helped dry venison and moose and have eaten my weight in both. Our daughter Penny dried beef one year. The beef's name, when alive, was Rumpelstiltskin and we called it Rumpel jerky. Penny experimented with the beef for a Science Fair project. We ate her project and she had to cure a second batch for the show. It was good.

Remove the fat (which tends to turn rancid) and the bone; cut the muscles of meat lengthwise and then across the grain. For a uniform cure, most pieces should be cut approximately the same size; beef jerky is cut into one-and-one-half-inch square strips of meat for a quicker cure and convenience of eating when traveling. Alaskans and farm families dried meat in larger pieces.

The first step in curing beef for drying is to weigh the meat and rub each piece with plain salt, using the ratio of ten to one (ten pounds meat to one pound of salt). The meat is layered in a crock with the surplus salt, weighted and left in a cool place for four days. It is then covered with a liquid consisting of one cup sugar and four teaspoons of saltpeter dissolved in one-half gallon of water.

Leave the meat in cure one-and-a-half days to the pound and, to insure a "good take," reposition it every few days. After the time in cure is completed, each piece is rinsed and hung to dry in a cool airy place for a week. Some people hot smoke their beef jerky but smoking is not necessary. Jerky may be eaten at once or wrapped and held in a cool place.

If meat is not dried properly, or if it is stored in a damp place, it is likely to mold. My grandmother would say that a little mold won't hurt, then she would wash it off with vinegar. But I knew a toothless old miner near Eagle, Alaska, who kept his dried caribou in a cave, and he had the hairiest meat I ever saw. His caribou squares grew two inches of fuzzy beard and he merely trimmed it off, smacked his lips, and gummed it.

Dried beef or game may be soaked to leach the salt, then cooked as fresh meat, or it may be cut very thinly and eaten raw or in a cream sauce.

When I was fourteen I slipped in the bathtub and knocked out my front teeth, a serious blow to my vanity. But, as someone said, "It's an ill blow that does not carry some good."

To recover my ego and await my new teeth, I was sent to a nearby farm, where sheep were raised. My grandfather would allow no "mutton" in his house, and although Grandma never bought lamb, in the pre-standardized days of the thirties sheep meat sometimes sneaked into store-bought sausage. At the first whiff of mutton, Granddaddy's proboscis would turn crimson and quiver. Next he'd rub his nose and blow it vigorously, and finally he'd empty all the meat in the garbage. I never knowingly tasted lamb until I was sent to the farm. It was then I discovered that I loved the country, and that I loved lamb chops, stew, legs and patty meat. But I especially remember the sweet pickled lamb shoulder.

Before he married the widow, who was owner of the handsome farm and 250 head of sheep, the farmer had been a meat cutter, and while I was on their farm he prepared a boneless rolled shoulder that I think even my grandfather would have enjoyed—if he could have kept his nose from itching. Pickled shoulder, the lamb was called.

For sweet pickle cure, use any large cut of boneless lamb. Remove the fat and cover the meat with a pickle made with two pounds of commercial dry cure salt to one gallon of water. It is important to cure fresh lamb at 36° to 38° F. to retard spoilage, and to overhaul and change its position every third day. Allow the lamb to remain in the cure for three days per pound and when the time is up, rinse the meat in clear water and hang it to dry in a cool place. Cured lamb tends to dry rapidly so it should be wrapped securely in muslin and several brown papers as soon as the surface dampness has evaporated.

My farm friends soaked their shoulders five hours in cold water before rubbing them with lard, onions, a little cloves, pepper, and nutmeg and roasting them in moist heat. The butcher-turned-farmer made wine as a hobby and he cooked the lamb in a pale apple wine. At the end of the cooking period he basted the meat with the sweet-tart juices. Served with baby turnips and potatoes, green peas and heaps of wilted lettuce, his pickled shoulder was delicious.

I have read that cured lamb may be smoked in the same manner as cured pork, held in hardwood smoke at 90° F. for two or three days until a tawny color develops.

Lamb ham is a popular English dish that reminds me of a good quality Canadian bacon. The hindquarters are trimmed and rubbed with a mixture of one cup of salt, one-third cup of sugar, one-and-a-half teaspoons of saltpeter. Care should be taken to stuff the cure around the bone and to rub it well into the meat. Fit the salted lamb into a container and make sure that all surfaces are covered with cure. Overhaul the meat every two or three days for two weeks, rubbing it well with the pickle that forms, then remove it from the crock, rinse it in cold water and hang it to dry. If the lamb ham is to be eaten soon after it is taken from the cure, soak it for one hour; if it has dried for a longer period, more time in soaking will be required to rid it of salt and to moisten the meat.

The initial cooking of lamb ham is by boiling for from two

to four hours, or until tender, then it is stripped with bacon and glazed for thirty minutes in a 375° F. oven. Sometimes a nutmeg, a teaspoon of whole cloves and a teaspoon of peppercorns are boiled with the ham to impart a spicy flavor, but I boil our ham plain and serve it with dill sauce. (Blend two tablespoons butter with two of flour and a half-cup of the water in which the lamb boiled. Cook until smooth and thickened, add one tablespoon of chopped dill and stir in one-half cup of sour cream.) The dilly cream compliments the mildly wild flavor of lamb ham.

Most game meat may be salt cured, smoked or dried in much the same manner as domestic meats. One difference, however, is that game fat is likely to be strong-tasting; for that reason, trim all game fat from meat to be cured. Fat such as cooking oil, butter or lard may be added to the meat when cooking it. With proper field dressing, chilling and cleanliness, game meat may be cured into excellent hams or jerky.

One winter I landed at a mine in the shadow of Mount McKinley. The two brothers who operated it had notified their parents that they had taken four caribou and that the meat was "ready to fly." Because I boarded at the parents' house in Anchorage, I volunteered to haul the caribou. Unseasonably warm weather had hit central Alaska and instead of frozen carcasses, nearly overripe meat had to be transported.

Thick clouds were sitting on the mountaintops as my stiff, smelly passengers and I labored with the plane for altitude. After several attempts to cross the shrouded peaks, I turned back and spent two weeks waiting for weather and helping cure caribou.

Luckily there was saltpeter, salt and sugar at the mine. We dry-rubbed the largest cuts, packed them in dynamite boxes, and overhauled them every third day. Thin cuts and bony pieces were sufficiently cured in ten days to rinse, hang and dry. The day before I left we smoked the shoulders and hams together with multitudes of loins. Although the meat was not fully cured, the weather turned cold and so it did not spoil. Once in a while since then I have purchased smoked pork chops that remind me of mildly cured, pink caribou meat.

Black bear meat cures beautifully, too, but as with other game all fat should be removed. And, since bears are a product of what they eat, cured meat from a fish-eating bear tastes like tough chunks of geriatric herring. Attention should also be paid to the bear's sex life; the meat of male bears in rutting season is awful.

There was a man on the Kenai who soaked moose meat in vinegar (half vinegar, half water) before putting it in cure. He said vinegar removed moose musk and tenderized the meat.

Whether you are partial to a vinegar bath, cold smoke, the dried, pickled or jerked process, moose and other wild meats gather zip and individuality when they take the cure.

4

Some End Up in Sausage

Sausage Queen of Twelfth Street—my grandmother enjoyed her title when we lived in St. Joseph, Missouri; but when I asked for her recipe she'd wink a Swiss blue eye and say, "If you know too much you'll get old too soon." Sometimes, as she popped spices into the meat, she would state, "Spice is the secret of a good life"; another time she'd declare, "Variety is vital to good humor." She never said the same thing twice nor did she make two batches of dried sausage alike.

I learned the three rules to her loose game of sausage-making, though: (1) good meat; (2) cleanliness; (3) adequate cure.

Dried or cured sausages are an independent lot and defy neat classification. Some of the sausages my grandmother made were fully cured and ready to eat; others were semi-cured and had to be refrigerated and cooked before they could be eaten. She made some sausages with wine and curing mixtures, others with cure and spices. Sometimes cured sausages were smoked, sometimes they were simply hung to dry. They came in all shapes and flavors, all textures and hardnesses.

My grandmother made sausage from bits and pieces of nearly every kind of meat. (She made Bunny Sausages the year rabbits overpopulated northwest Missouri.) Some of her sausages contained several varieties of meat, and she knew of one kind that was made with mule. We never tried it. We usually made our dried sausage out of pork when we butchered in the fall.

In some parts of the country folks look forward to hog killing like other people anticipate the World Series or the Superbowl. I remember a man in Missouri called Chief Sticker. For years I thought he was an Indian. As it turned out, he was the man called upon to kill hogs. "He keeps his sticker sharp from freeze-up 'till spring," a neighbor told me one butchering time. That's when I found out the Chief wasn't an Indian.

Neighbors often hauled their protesting pigs several miles to the killing spot near a running stream, and if the weather was not too fierce, kids were allowed to stay out of school to help carry wood and water.

Before dawn the butchering comrades had built a fire under the blackened, oversized bathtub where the pigs were scalded (140° to 150° F.) after their slaughter, and by sun-up the first pig was in the tank.

Scalding loosens the bristles, but if the water is too hot it "cooks the hair" and scraping becomes difficult. I remember one awful fight over temperature. By the time the shouting subsided, the hair was cooked and the two opponents glowered at each other over the carcass as they shaved the hog.

After scalding and scraping, the pig was hoisted by the hind leg tendons and hung from a "pole" or primitive A-frame to be cleaned and cooled. Hanging the pork on the pole usually took all hands plus a mule, if one was available.

When all squeals were silenced and neat pink porkers hung high on tripods, the men usually disappeared for a "bite." Upon their return, the butchering area was cleaned and the cutting proceeded on a four-foot-by-eight-foot plywood board. The head went first, with different people claiming the ears, jowl or lips. (We had a friend who refused to shoot his pigs, claiming it "messed up the brains," which he relished scrambled with eggs.)

Catching the fore half as the shoulder portion of the pig was cut down was always a test of strength for the young bucks at the hog killing. Cutting down and catching the hindquarters took every able-bodied man, and even then one or two were rolled by the meat.

After the four quarters, the chine and sides were trimmed, and the big pieces were allowed to cool overnight before being salted down. During the following five days fresh sausage, variety meats, lard, soap, and finally dried pork sausages such as Bratwurst or Italian links were created.

A special rule pertains to making pork sausage that is not to be cooked before eating: pre-freeze pork at minus-10° F. for twenty-one days. Trichinae, the disease-causing contaminant sometimes found in lean pork, are destroyed by prolonged freezing or by a thorough cooking.

Pork fat is used in most sausages (even sausages made with other kinds of meat) because pork fat is mellow and soft even when refrigerated. A total of 20 percent pork fat is the average amount called for, although some recipes call for 30 percent fat.

In making dried sausage, the shoulder, neck and side trimmings are usually ground, mixed with spices and stuffed into casings.

Ready-to-eat or semi-cured sausages may be stuffed into natural casing made from pig intestines, or into plastic or home-made muslin sleeves. Salted natural casings may be purchased from the butcher shop and are said to be superior because they encourage flavoring bacteria to grow on the meat. They must be soaked for a few minutes in warm water to wash out the salt, flushed clean, then shaken free of water before use. Man-made casings are bought from chemical companies and they may be softened by soaking them in warm water before working them onto the stuffing horn or your meat grinder. I sew unbleached muslin into sleeves or casings, sterilize them by boiling and work them onto the stuffing horn while they are wet.

Stuffing casings is an art. A sausage-stuffing attachment is most helpful. It is a little tube that fits on the food chopper and forces the meat through a funnel and into a casing. To stuff, force the prepared sausage into the stuffer attachment and slip as much soaked and rinsed casing over the attachment as it will hold. At this stage you will need seventeen fingers and two sets of teeth. In attempting to analyze and describe the sequence of stuffing I had to pick up three half-filled casings that shot across the kitchen and remove a loaded one from Lewis's boot. After which I decided to finish my stuffing without analysis and quote from the experts.

The operator supports the casing at the end of the stuffer with the first finger of his left hand while he turns the crank with his right hand. Pressing upward with the left forefinger and raising the stuffed casing above the end of the stuffer will pack the casing more tightly, thereby keeping out air pockets. Animal casings are cut after the proper-sized ring or length has been stuffed and a new length is then begun.

To tie the casings, drive a tenpenny nail into the far corner of the table and fasten it to one end of the stout, soft white string three feet long. Grasp both ends of the casing in the left hand and tie them together with two half hitches of string. . . .

Farmer's Bulletin No. 1186
GPO, USDA, Washington, D. C.

We do not make ring sausages, we merely stuff the casing the desired length and tie twice, that is, tie the sausage with string immediately next to the meat, leave about two inches of empty casing and tie a second time. Actually you learn to master stuffing about the time you run out of meat.

A commercial sausage stuffer is not absolutely necessary, Lewis decided one year when we had left our stuffer in the country. He cut off the bottom of a plastic gallon milk container, and the top and bottom of a six-ounce frozen juice can. He sterilized them both and taped the juice can over the pouring end of the milk bottle. Then he worked the prepared sausage casing onto the juice-can stuffing horn until it was tightly accordion-pleated, and with me holding the casing in place and helping to support the upside-down and bottomless milk carton that contained a couple of cups of sausage, together we stuffed. Lewis took a bamboo ramrod and, holding the milk container by its handle with one hand, he rammed the meat through the stuffing horn and into the casing with the other. Gradually he worked the casing off the horn as it became filled with meat. Forcing the meat tightly into place is important because air pockets in stuffed sausage encourage spoilage. A second important note is to check that the far end of your casing is tied or sewed. You don't want to go in one end and out the other. Some people squeeze their sausage into place by hand but I don't like to do that. It feels icky.

We try to tie most of our sausages in uniform lengths but with my sewing skill, some of our cloth-cased sausages end up three-inch peewees and some are chubby. Creating links with individuality may be some inner rebellion against standardized perfection, but we name our sausages, too. Hank's Tail was a squiggly salami, Marie's Folly was a wasp-waist delicacy, one fine wurst of well-endowed proportions was named after a hearty neighbor.

Other than stuffing, hanging or drying sausages is the most touchy part of the sausage game. Pork dries more slowly than beef or lamb but whatever meat is used, each length of sausage must be hung separately to dry in an airy, fly-free place with a temperature of about 55° F. for four days. This initial holding is called the green-room, fermenting or curing period. After the short green-room cure the sausage is stored in an airy, pest-proof place with a temperature of about 48° F. for a month or more. We have a screen storage box in the crawl space under our bedroom, and from time to time we crawl under the floor to see how our sausages are maturing. Air circulates through that dark, unheated area and as our sausages near eating time they become dry and hard. Sometimes a little harmless white mold forms on the outside of the casing. We merely wipe it off and forget it.

After sausage has matured and dried so that its flavor, texture and moisture content are proper, each sausage should be dipped in paraffin or rubbed with lard to seal it and preclude further drying. Hard sausages will become saltier and saltier and drier and drier until they are bitter salty chips of meat unless the drying action is stopped by sealing. Sealing, as in any of the natural processes of preserving, is a vital part of sausage making.

One of the simplest sausages to make and eat is Pork Summer Sausage, or Home Sausage as it was called at hog-killing time in my childhood. Contemporary sausage recipes often call for beef and pork trim meat, but years ago sausage makers utilized lean pork, or fatless wild meat plus regular pork trim in homemade dried sausages.

For Home Sausage (Pork Summer Sausage) chop or have your butcher twice grind six pounds of lean pork with four pounds of regular pork trim using a plate with three-sixteenth-inch holes on the first chopping and the one-eighth-inch-hole plate on the second go round. Pile the ground meat on a board or countertop. In a clean bowl mix by rubbing between your hands nine tablespoons of salt, four-and-a-half teaspoons black pepper, one scant teaspoon of saltpeter and one clove of chopped garlic. (Grandma used to add a little coriander, mustard seed or ground ginger for snappiness, and if Granddaddy passed through the kitchen he'd pour a cup of wine on the meat.) When the dry spices are thoroughly mixed, sprinkle them over the meat and work them well into the sausage. This is a cold operation; the saltpeter draws your skin and makes your fingers tingle, but after mixing Home Sausage you smell interesting for days. Some sausage makers grind their meat the second time after mixing in the spices.

Stuff Home Sausage into two-and-a-half-inch casings and tie them every eight inches with a stout string. Remember to tie the casings twice about two inches apart so that the sausages may be cut between the two ties; otherwise you will end up with one sausage tied and its brother hanging open on one end.

Hang the stuffed sausages in a dry, pest-free green-room area with a temperature of about 55° F. for about four days, then store the Home Sausage to dry in a pest-proof place with a temperature of about 48° F. for about a month. Taste one either sliced raw or chop one sausage with eggs for supper. If the dryness, flavor and texture are satisfactory you may seal it immediately with paraffin or lard. Or you may smoke your sausage at 110° F. for five or six hours, then raise the temperature slowly to 170° F. with a dense smoke for another hour and cool it gradually before sealing.

Home Sausage is equally fine food eaten raw in sandwiches or cooked. I remember a raggedy man yelling "Hot tamale!" as he pushed a cart through the streets of St. Joe. I always wanted to stop him but we didn't have many dimes, and when I'd ask, Grandma would reply, "I'll make you a tamale pie." It was an excellent all-in-one Home Sausage dish and a good way to clean out the icebox. My family loves it made with corned beef or hamburger, too.

Mix one-half cup of cornmeal, a pinch of parsley, chopped celery and onion if you have them, about four or five inches of chopped sausage, one cup of milk and three-fourths cup of water. Boil for about three minutes or until the mixture is thickened, stirring constantly. Add one slightly beaten egg, one-eighth teaspoon cumin, two teaspoons of chili powder, and salt and pepper to taste. Include any leftover vegetables such as corn or green beans (drained) and pour into a greased casserole. Arrange thinly sliced sausage over the top and bake in a moderate oven, 350° F., for fifteen minutes. Served piping hot with slices of crisp cold apples or quartered pears, Sausage Tamale Pie makes a delicious winter supper.

Garlic Sausage is a good pork sausage if you are partial to garlic. Lewis hates garlic, so we don't make this kind. But I helped make Garlic Sausage in Anchorage. A friend, a hog farmer, hung his sausages in the unheated cellar under his house. For many years it was his custom to break out sausages each spring after his "forty days' farewell to fat hams." Easter Sunday afternoon the whole western end of Anchorage smelled of garlic because he invited his neighbors to share his joyous day. Some people said his Garlic Sausage acted as their spring tonic—"Cleaned out stagnant pipes and pores." Others acclaimed it as their annual worming—"Purges the liver."

To make Garlic Sausage, grind ten pounds of lean pork such as Boston butt making sure that about two pounds of it is fat. In a dry bowl mix eight tablespoons of salt, one teaspoon of saltpeter, two teaspoons of black pepper and two-and-a-half teaspoons of allspice. When well mixed, add one teaspoon of coarse ground red pepper, six crushed or minced cloves of garlic and four teaspoons of fennel seeds. Mix a second time, then sprinkle over the meat and knead the spices into the meat with your hands for ten minutes. One-half cup of vodka or brandy is gradually worked into the sausage and two teaspoons of peppercorns are scattered through the meat. Mix the meat for another ten minutes and from time to time pause to sip brandy and warm your hands because all meat to be made into sausage should be held close to 38° F. while processing.

Stuff Garlic Sausage into two- or two-and-a-half-inch casings, pressing the meat firmly to insure a good take, and double tie into ten-inch lengths. Hang the sausages separately in an airy green-room area with a temperature of about 55° F. for four days. Store Garlic Sausage for two months by hanging in a cool, pest-free place with the temperature held at 48° F. Sausages and cured meats are said to mature best in 40° F. temperatures.

Ordinarily we taste our sausages after about four weeks to see how they are making out in the cool life, but since we never make Garlic Sausage I do not know whether it possesses precocious characteristics or not.

Italian Pork Sausage is a dried favorite in the New Jersey flatlands where my husband was reared. Combine seven pounds of lean pork and three pounds of fresh pork trimmings; grind it through the fine plate of the food chopper or ask your favorite Italian butcher to honor you with his chopper.

In a separate bowl thoroughly mix the following spices: eight tablespoons of salt, one-and-a-quarter teaspoons of saltpeter, four teaspoons of white pepper, one tablespoon of white sugar, one-and-a-half teaspoons of cardamon, one-and-a-half teaspoons of paprika, one-and-a-half teaspoons of nutmeg and one teaspoon of garlic powder.

Mix and sprinkle the spices on the ground pork. Knead by hand for twenty minutes.

Work one-half cup of red wine into the sausage for another few minutes and stuff into four-inch hog casings. Twist into twelve-inch lengths, tie securely and allow to dry in an airy pantry held at about 55° F. for four days. Hang Italian Sausage to dry for about two months at 48° F., or if you can't wait, sneak into the storage box after a month or so and nibble for a midnight snack. This is a great sausage eaten raw or cooked briefly on pizza.

I sew muslin sleeves for Italian Pork Sausage, cure them and seal each with a light brush of paraffin when the taste is perfect. I hang all my dried sausages in the cool screen box after they are sealed, but once I cut a sausage, I wrap it in wax paper and refrigerate it.

In contrast to dried pork sausage, which may be eaten raw or cooked, semi-cured pork sausage requires twenty to forty minutes of gentle cooking before it may be eaten. Semi-cured sausage may be smoked, half-smoked or dried to any degree desired. Some semi-cured sausages are given the green-room treatment, light smoked, then poached and eaten. Others are nearly dried before being cooked and eaten, but semi-dry pork sausages are not eaten raw. The traditional way of cooking semi-dry pork sausages is to boil them with greens and potatoes, but we enjoy the half-smoked, semi-cured sausages simmered with sauerkraut and served with a steaming bowl of potato soup.

Plain Sausage was my grandmother's everyday, semi-cured pork sausage. She simmered it with sauerkraut for forty minutes and served it heaped high like a haystack. For Plain Sausage, chop ten pounds of lean pork (one-fifth fat and four-fifths lean) through a medium plate. In a bowl, hand-mix nine tablespoons of salt, four teaspoons of pepper, a scant one-half teaspoon of cayenne pepper and a scant one-half teaspoon of saltpeter. Some people add a clove of garlic (crushed), others flavor Plain Sausage with a teaspoon of coriander seed, or mustard, or celery seed. The flavoring of these semi-cured sausages is often a deep, dark family secret. One neighbor in Missouri, who I think used anise seed, smiled a sweet mysterious smile when questioned about her spice. Her face told me she believed sausage flavoring to be a very private affair.

Work the spices into the meat, stuff tightly into two-inch natural casings and double-tie in five-inch lengths. Hang the sausages in a dry, airy 55° F. pantry for four days, then cool smoke, about 90° F. for four days. These Plain Sausages may be cooked and eaten at once or they may be kept in a cool place for poaching another day. Grandma did not seal Plain Sausage because she said the cool smoke tends to crust and prevents the sausage from excessive drying.

Bratwurst is another semi-cured sausage which should be gently boiled or cooked before eating. The recipe calls for the same amounts of pork, salt and saltpeter as the Plain Sausage, plus one tablespoon of celery seed, one teaspoon of mace and a pinch of crushed sage. My grandmother used to put four teaspoons of white pepper instead of black in Bratwurst. The white pepper seemed to impart a hotter flavor.

The sausages were stuffed, tied and pantry-cured like Plain Sausage, but the Bratwurst was smoked at a higher temperature, 120° to 130° F., for twelve hours or until it became as brown as an autumn oak. Bratwurst will keep well in a dry cool place, 40° to 50° F., and seems to bloom into a rich fullness with aging.

When I was a child, we neighborhood kids enjoyed going to the woods, building a fire and roasting potatoes. Mellow, mealy, white on the inside, burned black on the outside, campfire baked potatoes tasted especially good with Bratwurst cooked on a stick.

I have made venison sausage with several all-pork, semi-dry sausage recipes and used salt pork for fat. For some reason venison sausage was hard on the olfactory organs while hanging, but simmered in wine or beer, it tasted splendid. Game fat should not be used in sausage because it often seems tainted or offensive in taste. Wild meat should be pre-frozen before processing if the sausage is to be eaten uncooked. I have made Plain Sausage using moose and I have had bear Bratwurst, both pre-frozen and moistened with pork fat. The bearwurst would have been good if the bear had not lived on fish the last two months of his life, but ruddy, tough moose meat grinds its way into elegant cured products. Caribou and reindeer also may be ground, mixed with pork fat, spiced and fashioned into refined sausages. In fact, I believe reindeer rivals beef in hearty salamis. Although I have not tasted beaver, hedgehog or river rat sausage, I have heard of them and believe they could be made into some tantalizingly wicked wursts. Game, like other meats, should be killed and handled properly, seasoned and cured with care, then served with respect.

Pioneers of America created sausage from wild game, buffalo and deer. Farmers of the thirties generally made pork sausages. Today beef and lamb are also used, and homemade sausages containing a variety of meats are common.

Italian salami is often made with pork and beef, so when we slaughtered Rumpelstiltskin we utilized part of Rumpel's trimmings in salami.

First we opened a bottle of beer. This was to keep us out of our limited supply of the brandy which was needed to bind Rumpel's salami and to keep our spirits up.

We used four pounds of lean beef, three pounds of lean pork and three pounds of fat pork, all twice ground by the butcher. We put the ground meat on the countertop and Lewis kneaded about one cup of brandy into it while I mixed the salt and spices in a bowl. For ten pounds of meat we used nine tablespoons of salt, one-and-one-half tablespoons of sugar, one-half teaspoon ground white pepper, two tablespoons of coarsely ground black pepper, one scant teaspoon of saltpeter, one teaspoon of garlic powder and one teaspoon of coriander seeds. Because I was feeling expansive I also tossed in one-half teaspoon each of nutmeg and cardamon.

About the time I added the last spice I started choking and Lewis began to sneeze. We discovered one of the hazards of making salami. However, we learned that by soaking handkerchiefs in water and tying them bandit-style over our faces, we could minimize the sneezing and choking.

Thus protected we continued to add the spice to the meat. After a thorough mixing, we had begun to stuff the four-inch casings when a neighbor came to the door. Ours is a friendly house, and when Penny invited her in, our visitor came straight to the kitchen. Seeing my husband and me in kerchiefs ramming sausage into a muslin sleeve with a bamboo pole rather staggered her. Then the pepper got to her. Sneezing vigorously, she retreated into the dining room. There is nothing like a good sneeze to equalize the atmosphere.

I had made unbleached muslin casings for the salami because the larger natural or commercial casings were not available at the time. The cloth worked fine; we wet each sleeve in boiling water and worked it onto our homemade stuffer.

After tying the salamis into twelve-inch lengths, we rubbed the casings with a little salt and hung them in the basement, 55° F. for four days. Each salami was then hung in the screen box at about 48° F. At four weeks we tasted it—the meat was mildly flavored and moist but did not slice well; at eight weeks it was dried and had cured into a mature salami. To prevent further drying we brushed each sausage with paraffin and returned it to the cool, airy, screened box. When we cut a salami, we refrigerated the opened meat.

Pepperoni was a second Rumpel and pork sausage that Lewis and I made without smoking. Again we started with a cold beer because you need fortification and communion of spirit to co-operate with pepperoni. Sausage making is fun. We actually spent less than half a day putting down our various kinds of sausages this year, and that includes sprinting to the sewing machine and swishing up and down the seams of our un-bleached muslin casings. "It's not every sausage that gets a tailor-made sleeve," Marie commented as she helped sew casings to order.

For pepperoni we had our butcher grind seven pounds of un-seasoned, pre-frozen pork and three pounds of lean Rumpel. I mixed the spices and salt in a bowl with my hands while Lewis kneaded the cold meat and sterilized the utensils. The recipe called for nine tablespoons of salt, one tablespoon of sugar, one scant teaspoon of saltpeter, one tablespoon of cayenne, three tablespoons of paprika, one-half tablespoon of aniseed and one teaspoon of garlic powder. We mixed the spices and meat for one-quarter of an hour, or until our fingers were nearly frozen, because the temperature of the meat should be kept close to 38° F. Our hands took on a cherry color that lasted several days.

We stacked the loose pepperoni four inches deep in a pan to cure for forty-eight hours at 38° F. in the refrigerator. Finally we remixed the icy meat, stuffed it into two-inch pork casings and twin-linked it every ten inches. The sausage was hung to dry at 48° F. in the airy, dry, screened box for four weeks. Underaged pepperoni, like an underaged girl in a bar, is best not served. Rumpel's pepperoni looked so good and smelled so good that Lewis and I triumphantly gathered our friends and served it—what a disaster! Hotly spiced glucky hamburger. A month passed before we gained courage to try the pepperoni a second time; hesitantly we tasted a piece and it was great.

Usually associated with snacks, pepperoni dries into a solid meat. My family enjoys it on crackers after school, but we use most of our pepperoni on hearty suppers of pizza.

When making light bread, I usually grease some dough and save it in the icebox. A few hours before baking a pizza I take the bread dough out, beat it down and let it rise. I roll the dough very thin on a cookie sheet, spread each pizza with tomato paste and sauce (a can each, mixed), sprinkle it with oregano, a bit of Italian seasoning and garlic salt (if desired). I dot the pizza with lots of thinly sliced pepperoni, mozzarella cheese to web it together in a friendly fashion, and pop it into a 450° F. oven for fifteen minutes.

Homemade pepperoni on homemade pizza puts everyone in an energetic mood; we eat with our hands and talk and laugh as the hot cheese stretches. It's an easygoing meal. Sometimes we get into heated discussions. Recently we had a fine fight over high-sulphur fuels and thermal pollution, then ended up chewing on the concept of "growth is good." Someone pointed out that John Dewey had said that ideas concerning ethical questions must have their roots in natural explanations. What is the place and function of man in the environment? In the simplest terms we concluded that man must be faithful to the earth. That was a probing pepperoni pizza.

But I agree. Natural, saving points of view should be adopted wherever possible. Preserving meats by natural means is a molecular but positive way in which one man, one family, can wage war on waste. Sausage and bread, alone or combined in pizza, is simple fare that lends itself to relaxed yet stimulating exercises of the mind, and while gobbling it up young people often expound eye-opening ideas.

Holsteiner is an easy-to-make beef-and-pork sausage that is flavored by smoking. To six pounds of lean, ground beef add four pounds of pork sausage (about 50 percent fat), nine tablespoons of salt, four tablespoons of black pepper, two-and-a-half tablespoons of sugar and one scant teaspoon of saltpeter. Mix well and cure the bulk sausage for three days at 38° F. in a covered pan in a refrigerator. Stuff the cold sausage into muslin sleeves, four inches in diameter, and hang the sausage in greenroom temperatures, 55° F., overnight. Holsteiner is then cool smoked, 90° F., in a heavy smudge for two days, banked overnight (that is, laid on a solid surface with temperatures of about 48° F.) and hung to dry in an airy cool box for a month or two in temperatures of 48° F.

Mild and meaty, Holsteiner retains moisture and smoke flavor. It may be sliced thinly for sandwiches, chopped and cooked with kale and potatoes, or baked in Sausage Bread. My grandmother used to remove the casing and wrap hunks of presliced sausage in bread dough. She slashed the top of the big loaf diagonally three times, painted it with milk, sprinkled on a few sesame or poppy seeds and, after allowing it to rise, baked the loaf for forty-five minutes at 425° F.

Sometimes she sliced the warm (not hot) Sausage Bread and laid it on a plate, covered each slice with heated asparagus tips, then spooned a custard cream gravy over both. A daub of butter and a sprinkle of paprika or parsley made this an attractive dish.

Eaten warm or cold, served with or without gravy, Sausage Bread made with Holsteiner Sausage is a tasty surprise.

Kielbasa, or Polish Sausage, is a popular smoked sausage in our family. Three pounds of ground beef is mixed with seven pounds of coarsely ground pork. Too fine grinding of the pork is said to result in the dripping of the fat during the smoking, so a coarse, three-eighth-inch or larger plate should be used. The meat is seasoned with a mixture of one scant teaspoon of saltpeter, eight tablespoons of salt, three tablespoons of ground black pepper, two-and-a-half tablespoons of ground coriander and (for those who enjoy the garlic happiness) one-and-a-half tablespoons of garlic powder. For coarse-ground sausages, a second grinding to mix in the spices is not recommended, so after a thorough mixing the Polish sausage is pre-cured in bulk, or heaped four inches deep in a shallow pan and held at 38° F. overnight, then cased in two-and-a-half-inch hog casings. Some sausage makers hang Kielbasa in 55° F. for four days to set the meat before smoking, saying that this reduces shrinkage, but we smoke ours immediately after it is stuffed. Kielbasa, or Polish

Sausage, is smoked for twelve hours during which the temperature is raised slowly to 170° F. and held at that temperature until the color changes to a deep reddish brown. Hot smoked sausage should be cooled slowly, usually overnight, to prevent excessive wrinkling of the meat. Kielbasa is a semi-cured sausage and should be kept in the cool box (temperatures in the forties) and simmered gently before eating.

One time friends dropped in unexpectedly, and scratch as I did, I could dig up only one section of Polish Sausage. After it was cooked we all watched jealously to see that Lewis divided the sausage precisely into nine parts. Those tidbits of meat gave spark to our heaping platefuls of vegetables, and since then when those friends visit we serve Kielbasa just to relive that happy day.

Semi-dried sausages such as Mettwurst and Kielbasa should be hung in an airy cool box, or wrapped in wax paper and refrigerated, and cooked before eating.

Knackwurst, my grandmother's semi-cured beef-and-pork sausage, needed little preparation other than a brief poaching to bring out its musty flavor. She finely ground three-and-one-half pounds of lean beef and mixed it with six-and-one-half pounds of pork sausage. She worked in one cup of Rhine wine (or potato wine) with her hands and added the pre-mixed cure and spice: eight tablespoons of salt, one scant teaspoon of saltpeter, two crushed cloves of garlic, one tablespoon of black pepper, two tablespoons of paprika and three tablespoons of crushed cumin seeds.

Knackwurst is a soft sausage so it should be mashed, beat, and kneaded before stuffing into two-inch natural casings. Double-tie the sausages into five-inch lengths and hang them to cure at 55° F. for four days. Smoke Knackwurst for twelve hours in a light, cool smoke, 90° F., and refrigerate when cool. These little squiggles come by the yard and may be cooked without further curing; they are sassy when simmered in kraut and they are super-sausages when poached in a lidded skillet with a skim of water, then browned with the lid removed the last minute or two before serving. My family likes garlicless Knackwurst dropped into the bean pot when the dried kidney beans are almost mellow soft and ready to absorb the smoky cumin sausage flavor.

Whether you mix beef and pork in sausage, make bootleg

bear- or moosewursts, or indulge your whims to create venison salami, sausage making is an artistic way to preserve surplus and often less-than-prime cuts of meat.

Like people at a party, sausages respond delightfully to a drop of spirits, a little spice and attention. Smoky settings also enhance the hidden qualities of both people and sausages; sometimes a depth of character, or an unexpected tenderness is exposed in secret, hazy meetings.

5

Go Native with Tea

"Tea is glad and joyful," the one-armed river Eskimo said, inviting me into her cabin to talk about her daughter Phoebe. I had been with Phoebe when she died and had traveled to the lower Yukon to see her mother. I noted that the slender, timid Eskimo was a double for my former student. As she stirred the fire and set out cups and a basket of dried leaves, she apologized saying, "Only Labrador tea." I in turn apologized because I had brought nothing with me except memories of her daughter.

We talked and cried and sipped the spicy, aromatic tea. Somehow, its bright, gentle goodness reminded me of Phoebe, who had contracted tubercular meningitis a few months earlier.

We had not yet finished our first cup of tea when the children of the village crowded the doorway to see "Phoebe's teacher." Mothers came, old women questioned me, and again and again teacups were filled and the story of Phoebe's life at the boarding school and her death in the sanitarium was repeated.

Long after the sun had swung to the south and was circling the horizon northward, long after the day-lit night had turned into morning, villagers continued to stop at the cabin for tea and to extend their sympathies to Phoebe's mother. At last, completely saturated with details about the child who had been sent to "school" as the most select of their young villagers, the people left Phoebe's mother and me to sip one last cup of Labrador tea before sleep.

As I settled for rest I thought of the primitive custom of prob-ing, gently digging into painful memories, hurting, meaning to open wounds. Was this a premeditated effort to externalize and accept a distressful fact? Tea had played a part in the ritual, too; discussions about gathering, drying, and infusing it made up the small talk before the villagers asked about Phoebe; serving tea completed the ritual.

The following day when my plane cut the stillness of the muskeg country and we were circling aloft, I watched the tiny group of villagers waving from the river bank and I saw them fold around Phoebe's mother, supporting and sharing her need.

"Tea is glad and joyful." The shy Eskimo's words have stayed with me.

Before Chinese teas became popular, a great variety of native herbs were infused in liquid and drunk as tea. Some teas were taken for medicinal purposes; they were decocted from toxic and poisonous plants as well as from harmless herbs and drunk in an effort to change a physical or mental condition, to stimu-late, relieve pain, destroy vermin and virus, reduce fever, relax, coagulate and purge. People of early America turned to native medicinal teas because few doctors were available.

Some teas were thought to bestow specific virtues on the drinker. Frank Halman, a Missouri farmer who studies alma-nacs, gathered native teas by the moon signs. He believed that teas gathered and preserved under the different constellations would pass on the zodiac characteristics to the drinker. For ex-ample, tea herbs gathered under Cancer (June 21 to July 22) would pass on a productive quality to the mind. Mr. Halman had this worked out so that when he felt the need of a specific virtue, he'd drink a certain astrologically-gathered tea.

Most teas, however, are brewed and drunk for pure pleasure.

Erasmus Darwin, in 1800, wrote that tea "contributed to the health of the inhabitants of this island [England] by decreasing the potation of fermented or spirituous liquors; and to their mo-rality by more frequently mixing the ladies and gentlemen in the same society."

I have experimented with native teas for many years, and, though I cannot vouch for health- or virtue-giving qualities, I have brewed some exciting concoctions. On the other hand, some of my wild teas were evil-tasting and others were down-right nauseating. The greatest merit in native teas is the fun of prowling woods, fields and abandoned kitchen gardens in search of tea herbs. Sometimes the searching results in new tea tastes; sometimes the flavors that you find knock at half-forgotten doors to memories of other times and places. Foraging for herb teas and sipping them can be an ever-expanding pursuit.

Leaf, bud, fruit, bloom, root, bark or sap, it is important to gather tea makings at the time of year when their oils, fra-grance and color are at their peak.

To collect teas, herbs should be gathered after the dew or rain has dried but before the sun becomes hot. Aromatic odors and flavors of tea herbs are at their best when their leaves and blos-soms are at their prime. Only the greenest leaves and perfect blossoms which have just opened should be picked. Withered, heavy or insect-infested herbs should not be gathered and care should be taken that harvested plants are clean and free from insecticides.

When different herbs, such as elder, birch, persimmon and New Jersey tea leaves, are gathered at the same time, they should be sorted into individual containers at the time of cut-ting. I carry a grocery sack with several smaller brown paper bags folded open inside it. Herbs should be cut, not pulled, be-cause stripping bruises the leaf and thus flavors are released. Also stripping leaves from the branches damages the plant.

Just as Homer wrote that it is wrong to exult over slain men, so is it wrong to feel triumphant in gathering if a plant is de-stroyed. Even the least of our plants are very much part of our earth, and it is the responsibility of man with his intellect and will to protect and preserve them. Cutting herbs so as not to damage the plant is a small but important way in which man can substantiate his place and function in the environment.

Properly cured herbs—those that retain color, fragrance and oils—result from quick drying in a partially shady, airy en-vironment. Drying leaves should be stirred and turned daily. If the herbs have been cut into branch lengths, these should be bundled loosely and hung to dry. Most tea herbs dry in from four to ten days.

Mr. Halman hung his herb branches, or laid his leaf frames

under an arbor, but sometimes he spread the leaves in thin layers on brown paper in the warming ovens above the cook stove. Intense heat should be avoided, he told me, and air should be able to circulate around the herbs. Oven drying is not usually recommended for tea leaves because of the difficulty in controlling heat (too much heat or sun destroys color and oils); however, Mr. Halman said that a very brief 100° F. oven treatment after the leaves are dried discourages insects and molds. The crisp dried leaves should be crumbled and stored in clean, dry coffee tins that have been lined with brown paper. Do not use plastic bags. I did once and the tea leaves looked appealing until they turned into a dark and slimy kraut.

My grandmother dipped her wild tea branches in and out of boiling water immediately after they had been gathered. She did not oven-process the herbs after they had been dried, but she did crumble the dried leaves just as Mr. Halman did and stored them in labeled airtight containers.

Blossom drying takes greater care than leaves. Too much light or heat destroys the color and fragrance of blooms. Flowers should be cut when they are just beginning to open and spread quite far apart on mesh, such as cut-open nylon stockings, then laid in a cool, dark, dry closet. The flowers should be kept separated and turned daily. When dry, the petals should be removed and spread to cure for two or three days before storing. Mr. Halman did not oven-process flower tea.

Seeds are even more difficult to process than flowers. The seed stalks must be cut at precisely the proper time or whoosh! they scatter faster than a fidgety flock of flickers. Even after capture, seeds are not safe. Freeloading rodents and birds have a way of notifying each other of a feast, and they particularly enjoy chaff-free, picked-over seeds. Though seeds which have matured and dried on the plant need relatively little additional drying, they should be oven-treated at 100° F. for a few minutes, after which they may be stored in tightly lidded jars.

Roots, such as dock, are trimmed, washed, and sliced lengthwise to hasten drying and minimize molding. Dug whole after the leaves of the plant are full-grown, roots should be rinsed thoroughly, sliced, spread one layer thick on screens and dried in a shed or closet. As they shrink, they should be turned every day, and when still pliable but not moist, root pieces should be cured in a low oven, 100° F., for ten minutes. A second week of shelf drying is often necessary before they become brittle and are ready for storage in a container with an airtight lid.

In digging roots, as in other herb gathering, it is of utmost importance to identify the plant. Many species may easily be confused with harmful plants. This is especially true with regard to roots. Numerous roots are violently poisonous. Exact identification is imperative when harvesting all native teas. Identify herbs by their botanical names, because local names change from place to place.

I remember a Frenchman in Alaska who literally threw himself into a patch of evergreen perennial, shouting "Rheumatism root!" Our companion, a native Alaskan, agreed, and together they built a fire and infused a strong tea. The Frenchman gulped down a cup of the blackish-green brew, smacked his lips, cried "Delicious!" and promptly passed out. The Indian and I carried him three-and-a-half miles to the highway, flagged a jeep, stuffed him into it and, hanging onto fenders and hood, rushed him to the hospital. He almost died. The herb he referred to as rheumatism root was a local medicine for bone aches. The Indian said his people rubbed it on the sore spot. The Frenchman told the doctor he thought the plant was an aphrodisiac discreetly called rheumatism root as a cover.

Remember, too, collect only those roots, seeds, flowers or herbs that you can use. Gather in an area where the plant grows in profusion and collect tea materials with the idea of thinning or trimming. Do not take all of the roots available or all of the seeds. Wild plants must propagate themselves. To strip an area is to destroy your own source for years to come.

Beware of mixing your own blend of wild tea. Some herbal extracts are powerful, and when used by themselves are beneficial, but mixed with other herbs they can be harmful.

To infuse tea, pour boiling water over the dried or fresh herb and steep the tea for five to fifteen minutes. Most native teas may then be strained and drunk. Unless specified, do not boil teas, because boiling may draw out bitterness or pernicious substances. A teaspoonful of tea leaves, buds, flowers, bark or root per teacup of water is usually suggested. Sugar, honey, cream or lemon may be added for more allure.

Alphabetically listed below are some fair and foul teas. Some are fun drinks, others are reliable beverages, one or two are curious conversation teasers.

Go Native with Tea

ALDER, SWAMP ALDER BARK TEA (*Alnus rubra*), gathered by peeling at any time of the year, is a bitter red-brown drink that is said to quench thirst and build blood. I have drunk alder tea by accident. Once I melted snow in the alders and the liquid contained bits and pieces of alder bark that had been worked loose by moose who eat the stuff. I thought it was alder-flavored water, but later my girlfriend teased that it might have been the moose who flavored it.

AVENS (*Geum urbanum* and *G. rivale*) has a history of comforting the heart. In Europe during the sixteenth century, a fashionable tea called Holy Herb was infused from the whole avens plant. Avens plants and roots were gathered in July while the nodding flowers were at their peak; the whole herb was dried by bunching loosely and hanging in a shaded area, then the leaves and flowers were stripped from their coarse stalks and crushed. The tea was said to cool fevers and heated throats. More recently, in America, avens roots have been boiled into a weak, chocolate-like tea. I have dug avens roots in the fall, boiled them, and drunk the infusion after adding cream and sugar. It was terrible. Avens root tea may comfort the heart but it does little for the gullet. I have read, however, that dried avens root protects clothing from moths, so if you despise the tea, sprinkle the root among your woolens.

BEARBERRY, KINNIKINIK (*Arctostaphylos, uva ursi*) is a leathery-leafed little plant that is said to brew into a tea for digestive troubles. One summer when I was cooking in a mining camp near Rampart on the Yukon River, I also helped to run waterfowl into penning areas for banding. The Fish and Wildlife biologists called the operation "catching them with their feathers down" because the banding of geese and ducks had to be accomplished during molting season. As I loped across the muskeg after a willful, frizzle-feathered flock of honkers, a bandy-legged Indian ran toward me, his legs pumping like a bicycle rider's. He stopped squarely in my path. Then, "You come," he panted. Explaining that my birds were scattering, I tried to move after them but he grabbed my elbow and emphatically repeated his demand.

I was the only woman at the bird-banding. Believing the man's wife to be in need of feminine assistance, I called to my fellow herders and followed the Indian. We traveled steadily for over an hour before we came to the river bank on which was pitched a desolately ragged tent. Inside sat a squaw, rigid. Her eyes were open but she did not blink; the motionless black spheres seemed suspended in liquid as they stared toward the open flap. There was no recognition or expression on her face.

"Kinnikinik," the man said matter-of-factly. At first I thought the word was her name; then I remembered Kinnikinik leaf tobacco, which was occasionally smoked by the natives of the tundra. When Kinnikinik tobacco was combined with alcohol, the effect was said to be powerfully potent. The woman was stoned!

As I backed from the loathsome, stinking place, a movement in the dark corner of the tent caught my eye.

"David. You help David," the man said when I paused.

He brought the skinny, bulging-bellied three-year-old to me at the river bank where I had retreated for air. The child's large eyes were stoical with fright and I saw that a rusty three-pronged fishhook protruded from the nail of his tiny filthy thumb. The squat man held out a razor to me. His face depicted such pleading and helplessness that I was hypnotized. With movements so rehearsed and fluid that I actually seemed to be guided by some hypnotic direction, I burned the blade and cut the nail lengthwise along the side of the hook, then pushed the fishhook backward and out. The baby screamed, the mother staggered from the tent, and the man bowed his thanks as the thumb spurted blood. It was a wonder I didn't faint.

Later I learned from the same tribe of Kuchin Indians that "a father cannot make his own son tough." In their native culture the maternal uncle performed emergency and health care duties. It was the uncle's role to discipline and train his nephew too. A father who could not by tradition make his own son tough, in turn trained and cared for his sister's sons. Because of invasions of disease, alcohol and other cultures, many maternal uncles of the Kuchin were gone. The father who ran to me for help was restricted by his tribal mores and was unable to help his own son. The mother escaped the confusing world through "Kinnikinik."

Today, I cannot read the name bearberry or Kinnikinik without remembering the devastated Kuchin of Alaska.

NORTHERN BEARBERRIES (*A. uva ursi, A. alpina* and *A. rubra*) are greedily eaten by bears, ptarmigan and, as an emergency food, by people, and the dried leaves are infused into tea and drunk both as a hot beverage and as an aid to digestive upsets. The tough little leaves are gathered in September, spread out singly in a warm shed and dried quickly. I do not know about the medicinal qualities of bearberry leaves, but as a tea this mild-flavored drink is pleasant.

Bergamot, Oswego tea (*Monarda didyma*, Labiatae family) has a sunny disposition. Its unkempt crimson flowers attract multitudes of bees, but the young bergamot leaves are picked in June or early July before the herb blooms. Some people cut the whole, square-stemmed plant for drying, but others harvest only the leaves. Some people drink bergamot tea for bronchial ailments or to inhibit pregnancy. I enjoy a cup of Oswego tea just for the pleasure of its zippy taste.

Birch, known as sweet, black or cherry birch (*Betula lenta*), brews into a fragrant wintergreen-flavored tea that is a favorite in our house. Sweet birch contains oil-bearing twigs and leaves that may be infused fresh in June or picked and dried and stored for a fragrant winter tea. The vagabond birches lead carefree lives and clothe the earth with beauty where they grow. *Betula lenta*'s deep-colored, satiny bark seems to set the sweet birch aglow with life even during the dead of winter. Abruptly, each April, impatient catkins tassel. Later, glossy bright leaves announce to the woodland that the time for birch tea harvest has returned.

Native peoples of the North strip inner bark from sweet birch and dry the long shreds for winter use as tea. In Alaska, I met Aleuts who said their ancestors traded seal skins for Kamchatkan "sweet bark" and the Aleuts wove some of the fragrant fiber into delicate baskets. Other natives told me that their grandmothers boiled the birch bark with fish, and they grinned joyously as they described its spicy goodness. Pioneers in America cut sweet birch twigs and made a strong infusion which contained salicylic acid and was used to treat rheumatism. Although I cannot vouch for beautiful *Betula lenta*'s medicinal or fish-flavoring qualities, as a tea I have found it superb.

Boneset, Joepye, thoroughwort (*Eupatorium perfoliatum*) is a crazy-leggy perennial that produces flat-headed, hairy purplish flowers late in the fall and provides one last nip for the road for tardy autumn butterflies. Around Culpeper, Virginia, mountain families gather thoroughwort flowering tops and boil them into digestive decoctions. These preparations are said to restore body tone. They also collect the young leaves each spring and brew a fresh tea which is used to treat coughs and constipation. Although the literature lauds its medicinal qualities, and our Apple Tree Lane is loaded with Joepye weed (named for an Indian who earned fame by curing "horrors" with this plant), we have not indulged in the *Eupatorium* happiness.

BORAGE (*Borago officinalis*), a low-down relative of common comfrey, was known as one of the four cardinal flowers in ancient herb classifications. Fresh borage flowers infused in wine were believed to bestow the virtue of courage on the consumer. More recent studies indicate that the salts present in the fresh flowers may be activators, but the fearlessness attributed to the early-day borage tea was probably psychological. Fresh borage flowers have been used in salads to "make the mind glad," and some good Puritans dried the blue and white flowers for a winter tea "to drive away sadness." Whether or not consumption of borage flowers makes a man merry, the bold borage plant is cheery in appearance and its cooling, cucumber-like quality adds joy to drinks.

BURDOCK ROOT TEA (*Arctium lappa*) gathered in the fall, dried, and infused for ten minutes in boiling water, was drunk by a family I knew "to cleanse the blood and stimulate the functions." I have never clearly understood what they meant, so I have never tasted burdock root tea.

CHAMOMILE (*Anthemis nobilis*) is a noble old medicinal flower. My grandmother used to make "chamomile" tea from dried, apple-scented daisy flowers which she brewed as a cure for stomachache. One year I decided to skip through the meadow and snatch Mayweeds (*Anthemis cotula*), thinking I would brew some tea. Yeck! Mayweed may be a chamomile cousin, but it's a smelly kin. I could not pick it.

CHICKWEED (*Stellaria media*), a plant that mothers its young shoots by folding larger leaves over tender stalks, is readily consumed by chickens and by country people who enjoy tea made from chickweed leaves. Whether infused from fresh or dried leaves, farm folk say "chick tea" soothes the senses.

DOCK (*Rumex aquaticus* or *Crispus*) is credited as beneficial to skin troubles when the roots are washed, shaved, dried until brittle, then infused with boiling water to make tea. Last spring I dug for one-half hour on a root as big as my forearm intending to try the herb tea on my teen-agers. I worked up a sweat which probably benefited my pores, but that dock root is still in the ground.

ELDER (*Sambucus canadensis*) leaves or flowers have long been associated with rural magic. If you feel the need for a pick-me-up because of heavy plowing through the children's rooms or suburban traffic, visit low pastures and gather elder blossoms or leaves in June or July. The broad, ill-smelling, creamy white umbels, steeped in boiling water overnight, then strained and drunk the following day, make a heady, invigorating, ugly-tasting drink. Actually, after the first glass, it doesn't taste so bad and it seems to make your heart beat faster and your outlook brighter.

Elder bloom clusters and young leaves may be dried in the shade for a winter tea, and although not quite so stimulating and evil-smelling as when fresh, brew into a warming tea.

EYEBRIGHT (*Euphrasia americana*), named Gladness by the ancient Greeks, is a petite plant that seems to smile at you with its tiny white and violet snapdragon flowers. The whole plant is gathered while blooming June until September, dried and crumpled for morning tea. Mirth seems to be embodied in eyebright's agreeable flavor.

FENNEL SEED TEA (*Foeniculum vulgare*) was a remedy used by my grandmother's neighbors for baby colic. They made fennel tea by boiling a cup of milk and adding one teaspoon of fennel seed. The milk was stirred for about a minute, then strained and given to the screaming babe as soon as possible. Mothers brought their miserable infants from blocks around for "seed tea and tonic." Tonic was a little warm wine given to the harassed mothers.

GOLDENROD, SWEET GOLDENROD (*Solidago odora*) was one of the first native teas commonly served in America. Both the smooth, spice-scented, lance-shaped leaves cut when young, and the flowers, gathered when fully expanded in July or August, may be dried, mixed and brewed into a pleasant tea with anise overtones. Blue Mountain tea, as sweet goldenrod tea is called in some areas, is a welcome change from China tea. Less expensive, too.

HOLLY, CASSINA, YAUPON is said to be the most desirable native substitute we have for Chinese tea, the one that tastes most like commercial tea. Unfortunately the botanical name, *Ilex vomitoria*, prejudices some people, but knowing folk from Florida to Texas bravely harvest the shiny new holly leaves each January when their oils are best and tannin least bitter. Dried and steeped in water, yaupon is said to be mildly stimulating and grandly refreshing.

Hops (*Humulus lupulus*) flowers and upper leaves are sometimes dried and infused for a few minutes in boiling water to create a quieting tea. One man told me he went one step further —he moistened hops with whiskey *and* hot water and drank this fortified hops tea as a remedy for wakefulness.

Horehound (*Marrubium*) and other members of the mint family are sometimes welcomed as a taste twist in other teas, but horehound is more often a liquid reject because of its objectionable odor. The whole mint family seems to be loaded with family skeletons. Mad-dog skullcap (*Scutellaria lateriflora*) once enjoyed the false reputation of curing hydrophobia. Creeping Charley (*Nepeta glechoma*) makes the most of its transvestite potential; first the flowers are male, later they change into females. *Nepeta cataria* could be the name of a house of ill-repute, but it really refers to a hairy, hoary plant that drives cats half-crazy with delight. Heal-all (*Prunella vulgaris*), with a cleft stigma, for years pretended to cure every fleshly ill before it was exposed as a hoax. Horse balm (*Collinsonia canadensis*), a mint-tasting phony, was once used alternately as a horse and human tonic. False dragonhead (*Physostegia virginiana*) tries to trick people into believing that it is a snappy snapdragon. And the king of con artists in the plant world, pennyroyal (*Hedeoma pulegioides*), is really a squaw mint with a very strong scent. Kennel owners sprinkle their kennels with pennyroyal leaves to kill fleas, an undignified end for a plant that claims to be royalty. Spear, pepper and other *Menthas* were, according to legend, metamorphosed beauties, rivals of Pluto's wife who were changed into mint plants and doomed to spend their lives enticing insects.

Skeletal heritage or not, to my taste mint leaves add a dash of fragrance to modern-day teas.

"Kink shrub," cinquefoil (*Potentilla fruticosa*) is a pretty yellow-flowering plant that grows about a foot tall amid rocks in central Alaska. The silky leaflets (actually small, compound leaves) are plucked by the handful in July and dried for a mild yet peppery tea. I brewed freshly gathered kink leaves in the base hills of Mount McKinley and carried some of the green tea part of the way up the mountain. Unfortunately my companions and I ran out of both steam and tea before we reached the big glacier and we did not make it to the top. Myths indicate that cinquefoil tea was dried and brewed by natives before the Russians explored Alaska, and recent findings show that this plant is a rich source of ascorbic acid.

KNOTGRASS TEA (*Polygonum*) was poured into me by the quart when I suddenly started sprouting toward my full height. Years ago, knotgrass was thought to stunt the growth of children so I was given the tea to drink. Although it did little to slow down my growth, I know I did my part to rid northwest Missouri of the noxious knotweed.

LABRADOR TEA (*Ledum decumbens, L. latifolium* and *L. groenlandicum*) grows in sub-Arctic muskegs. Both aboriginal peoples and pioneers gathered the heavy leaves during August for tea which was drunk throughout the year. Leaves of this low, aromatic shrub may be collected at any time, for foragers say the tannin and oils are most precipitant just before the flower clusters appear. In addition to drinking Labrador tea with Phoebe's mother, I have sipped *Ledum* while huddled before a roaring fire when ice fog lay thick on the flat lake country of Alaska; I have gulped it while firepotting a plane for takeoff in minus-zero-degree weather; and I have enjoyed it with friends before a rustic fireplace. To me, it bears little likeness to commercial products, but Labrador tea is a friendly drink.

LINDEN, BASSWOOD (*Tilia americana*), the stately tree associated with Linnaeus, blossoms into a profusion of honey-laden flowers which may be infused fresh (or dried) into a bland and quieting tea. I knew a dainty lady who brewed linden tea in Virginia each June when her hilltop tree showered the area with creamy blow. Reaching up into the perfumed branches, she would pinch off a cluster of the blooms, then cover them with boiling water. Sitting on her veranda, rocking, sipping fresh linden tea (which I like with cream and sugar), she was truly "the princess of Freedom Hill" as she narrated bits of the history of the surrounding land. How proud she was of her family's part in the life of early America. A poet once said that life is a dream of a shadow. The life of her linden tree cast a glorious shadow. Now the massive tree is gone. In its place a slab of blacktop sprouts shiny new cars and wild-tied salesmen. Their sales lot has entombed the roots of an American linden together with its memories and its patriotic tea.

"MAY TEA." Blossom teas are as old as the blooms of May. Apple, plum, honeysuckle or rose blossoms may be cut when in full flower, and steeped fresh in boiling water, or dried and infused into a delicate-flavored tea. My tea-drinking friend in Missouri declared that the bouquet of flowers was captured in tea and that it gave bloom to the spirit. He especially enjoyed rose tea but his wife took a dim view of his foraging in her rose garden. Today, however, with trigger-happy sprayers roaming the countryside, I hesitate to snip blossoms for tea. Arsenic on my tonsils is not the way I plan to go.

MOTHERWORT (*Leonurus cardiaca*), a kindly herb valued in the Middle Ages as a medicine for female disorders, may be harvested while in bloom from July to September. The whole plant may be cut and hung to dry. Later, the leaves and flowers are crumbled and stored for a tea to counteract womanly doldrums or, as they used to say, melancholy vapors. Bitter as gall, motherwort tea may be kindly to the vapors but it is harsh on the taste buds.

MUGWORT, ST. JOHN'S PLANT, WITCHES HERB (*Artemisia vulgaris*), a nervous ragged-looking plant, was associated with sorcery in the Middle Ages. It was believed that its common ragweed-like leaves always turned north. Mugwort was also considered to be a sort of patron saint of travelers. The story goes that to carry mugwort was to protect yourself against misfortune and tiredness. Picked while in flower, in July and August, the whole mugwort plant is dried in bunches and crumpled for tea. I have smelled the brew. That is as far as I could go. Mugwort tea has an odor like wet dog hair.

NETTLE, STINGING NETTLE (*Urtica dioica*) is a fiber, fodder, food, dye, fermented beverage and soil-building plant that seems to resent its reputation as a weed. For years it has tried to overcome this stigma by contributing its topmost leaves to teapots. During May and June, nettle tops are picked after a rain or when dew has softened their prickers. I have tasted nettle tea made from an infusion of dried young leaves and from sliced and dried nettle roots; both teas were excellent. For good nettle, nonmedicinal tea, gather nettle tops in June and hang them in bunches or spread the leaves on trays to dry; crumble and store.

If you pick the nettle tops early enough, flowers and seeds will sprout from the sides of the stalk. Thus you do not destroy an abundance of nettles for the future.

NEW JERSEY TEA, WILD SNOWBALL or RED ROOT (*Ceanothus americanus*) was the colonial housewives' answer to George III's tax. As they brewed the leaves which had been gathered and dried in early June, they could not help but feel proud of America's stand against an unjust tax. My grandmother used to immerse the fresh leaves in boiling water for one moment, then dry the branches in the shade. The tea made from dried and crumbled leaves had an agreeable tannic taste and coated the tongue with an interesting rough feeling.

PERSIMMON (*Diospyros virginiana*), familiar as a fruit, may also be utilized as a leaf tea substitute. I have picked the leaves in June and dried them, then in the winter enjoyed the full-flavored tea, which reminded me of northern spruce tea.

PLANTAIN (*Plantago*) tea was an old time mainstay each March for "rheumees and rotteness." I have not tasted tea made from dried plantain leaves, but they smell like peculiar hay.

POPLAR LEAF TEA (*Populus tremuloides*) used to be a popular tannic tea. The young white or aspen leaves were gathered, dried and infused as a pick-me-up during the winter.

PUMPKINS (*Cucurbita pepo*), the Indians' chief plant food after corn, contributed their seeds to the world of teas. Briefly roasted, pounded and steeped in boiling water, pumpkin seed tea served with milk and a bit of sugar or honey is a soothing and wholesome drink.

ROSE HIP or BRIAR TEA is a popular drink in Alaska. Rose hips are dried whole either by laying them on cloth in the sun or allowing them to dry on the bush. Competition with ptarmigan and titmice is less when hips are picked and dried at home. Older native men, I was told by a Nulato Indian, "drink briar tea for rocks in his canal." Everyone who has tasted the pink lemonade flavor of rose hips loves the tart, teasing taste. Native mothers on the Yukon simply boil a handful of the bright wild rose fruit for ten minutes, add a spoonful of sugar and serve the tea together with three or four rose hips in each cup. The fruit is nibbled after the cup is drained and children pucker, then giggle at each other's faces. Rose hip or briar tea is a happy beverage.

SAGE (*Salvia officinalis*) is a common tea leaf used in some parts of the country. It is also reputed to be an anthelmintic, which means "against the worm."

SASSAFRAS (*Sassafras officinalis*) is well known for its spicy, aromatic bark and root that may be infused in tea "to clear the blood" each spring. Available throughout the year, sassy tea may be made from fresh or dried roots or bark. I use the same strong-willed root over and over until all the red-brown color has been extracted and the taste tamed. I had a friend who dried and powdered young sassafras leaves and steeped them into a placid-looking tea.

SCURVY GRASS (*Cochlearia officinalis*) is a circumpolar seashore plant that is usually eaten as a succulent leafy additive to salads for its antiscorbutic qualities. Some coastal peoples brew fresh scurvy grass leaves into a bright tea. I was warmed by the peppery liquid one wet July when I was helping salt and smoke salmon at a fish camp in Alaska. I have never heard of tea being made of dried scurvy grass.

SORREL (*Rumex acetosa*) is similar to dock in flavor and has arrowhead leaves that may be cut in spring or early summer, dried and infused into a lightly acid-flavored drink. I have heard that tea made with fresh sorrel flowers contains less oxalic acid or sourness. Flavored with honey, sorrel leaf or flower tea is considered a soothing infusion, and country people used to drink it to help their digestion. I do not know about *Rumex*'s medicinal qualities but I can testify that it improves pucker power.

SPICEBUSH, WILD ALLSPICE (*Lindera benzoin*) brews into a quick, angry tea. Its full-grown leaves, gathered and dried in August, make an impatient drink. Allspice odors beg you to taste the tea, which then bites the tongue. Mr. Halman told me that spicebush tea transmitted an honest disposition to the drinker.

SPRUCE TEA. Throughout the sub-Arctic, "spruce tea" is made from an infusion of the young twigs and leaves of balsam fir, spruce, hemlock or pine. An antiscorbutic, spruce tea is steeped in boiling water and drunk with sugar.

SUMACH (*Rhus glabra*) is often downgraded because it grows so eagerly along ugly earth scars and road cuts, but to me sumach is a splendid beauty. I love to see the wind play in its lacy leaves and its cockscomb seeds redden in the fall. From the middle of August to September, the densely clustered, hairy fruit of

Rhus glabra may be snapped off before a rain and hung to dry. I have found that mice relish dried sumach berries, so it is best to hang the heads of fruit where the little thieves can't reach. Simply covered with boiling water, strained and sweetened, sumach fruit tea is tasty.

THISTLE (*Cirsium palustre*), I have read, may be infused into a fresh or dry leaf tea if the leaves are cut when young in the spring. Mild thistle leaf tea is said to strengthen the memory. I have often meant to indulge in thistles, but, though we have a pasture full of the spiny rosettes, I always forget to bring a knife to cut them when I walk through the open field.

VERVAIN, SIMPLER'S JOY (*Verbena officinalis*, *V. hastata*) has been the subject of folklore ever since the early Christians and Druids counted it among their healing plants. Simpling, an old term meaning the gathering of useful herbs (generally, plants which were not combined with other substances for medical virtues), gave this popular herb its common name. The whole plant was cut from June to August, dried, stripped from its coarse stalk and crumbled. Both leaves and flowers were mixed for tea. Verbena, the showy garden sister of dowdy-looking vervain, has been a traditional bridal flower, a symbol of chastity, which is curious because the *Verbenae* are among the few plants that readily exchange pollen with other species and might be classified as promiscuous flowers. Tea steeped from dried vervain leaves and flowers possesses a mildly bitter taste. Loose morals or not, vervain tea is quite palatable to most people.

VIOLET (*Viola odorata*) is a fragrant flower, which has been brewed into a favorite tea since the days of Hippocrates. Both flowers and leaves may be gathered in the spring, dried, stored and infused with boiling water for a pleasureful pause. I use three times as much delicately flavored violet tea as I do the regular Oriental varieties. With cream cheese and olive sandwiches, a fingerful of watercress and a bowl of celery soup, violet tea gives your taste buds a rest; a relaxing respite in today's world of hard-driving spices and sensations.

WILD MARJORAM (*Origanum vulgare*) and WILD THYME (*Thymus serpyllum*), cut and dried during their flowering periods from June to August, then rubbed from their stems and stored, give promise of quick personality teas throughout the winter. Unlike the violet tea, marjoram and thyme tea should be used sparingly; discretion is the rule for these wild-eyed herbs that are said to soothe that troublesome complaint: nightmare.

WITCH-HAZEL (*Hamamelis virginica*) is considered a valuable native tea when made with young, oil-heavy leaves that are collected and dried in June. Years ago Indians used to gather witch-hazel flowers in the fall. They believed that the spirit of the sun slept in the yellow squiggles, and after they dried them, they waited until a dark day, then boiled the flowers and drank the decoction "to make the sun come out." I have not tried the sunshine infusion, but pausing to sip a cup of hazel tea certainly restores a sunny disposition.

Preserving a bit of nature, a handful of leaves that you have identified, plucked and processed, gives a touch of the real to the plasticity of most of our lives. Preserving oddball teas, drying and storing them, is unbelievably simple, and, as with most natural life experiences, gives far more in return than the time and energy expended.

6

Fizzy Fun and Fortunate Coolers

"Happiness bubbles from within; fortune comes from without . . ." Bucke's principle certainly applies to bottled beverages. Sometimes there is so much happiness inside a bottle that it cannot contain itself and you have to scrape cork off the ceiling.

In reality, exploding fizzies are not much fun. There is always the danger of splintered glass. When I held my Cub Scout den meetings in our cellar, I barricaded our root beer in a corner using cardboard boxes. A neighbor uses a shield of screening for the temperamental brew.

A few years ago kitchens served as headquarters for home brewing as well as a preserving and retort center. Most homes contained large barrels, crocks and tubs for processing fruits; they had small lidded kettles for simmering extracts; there was a presser for fruit, a colander, some funnels, a siphoning apparatus and a variety of "Hippocras bags" or sacks to be used for fine straining. Bottles, lids, corks, caps, a bottle capper, a paraffin can and a sterilizer or wash boiler were ordinary utensils of the home.

"Cosmetics change a lady's skin, but not her habits," my grandparents said over and over as they tried to inspire me to neatness. Now I see that they were products of habit. Because they had emigrated from Europe where it was often dangerous to drink plain water, they made light beer from anything handy out of habit. Around my grandfather's house, water was something to wash in, to carry to the chicken yard, and to hose yourself down with in hot weather.

As my grandfather explained it, home-fermented wines, beers, light beers and soft drinks undergo a similar process: they all are created out of a mixture of liquid, sugar, nutrients, flavoring and yeast. Brewer's or wine yeast, fresh or dried baker's yeast, or homemade starters from yeast-brewed commercial beer may be used. Yeasts are tiny plants which feed on sugar and give off alcohol and fizz. The fizzies are gas-filled bubbles; the gas is carbon dioxide. In order to grow and produce fizz, the yeast must have food, oxygen and warmth.

For wine, sweetened liquid and yeasts are encouraged to ferment until the alcohol content becomes high enough to inhibit further yeast growth. The fermenting action of most wines is allowed to run its course and the wine is "locked" or bottled when bubble-less. Wine usually stops the yeast action when the alcohol content is about 14 percent by volume.

In making malt beer, the yeasts are allowed to grow in sweetened and flavored liquid and to produce alcohol and fizz, but home-brewed beers are bottled before the fermenting action has completely stopped. Thus, beers retain some carbon dioxide bubbles. Home-brewed beers are generally not as alcoholic as wine because beer recipes do not use as much sugar and not all of the sugar is converted before sealing.

Soft drinks and light beers call for even less sugar in the flavored liquid and the yeasts are permitted only a brief time in which to grow and produce fizz and alcohol. Soft beers are bottled shortly after mixing; thus the oxygen supply is cut off and the yeasts cannot do their thing.

Commercial soft drink manufacturers put bubbles into beverages with liquid carbon dioxide. Although carbon-dioxide-making apparatus is available, true home-brewed drinks are made bubbly with yeast and sugar. Because yeast and sugar produce alcohol as well as fizz, homemade soft drinks are likely to be a little hard. The trick is to stop the yeast/sugar reaction before much of the sugar is turned into alcohol by the yeast. A good home brewer, like a good cop, has an educated eyeball that can spot and stop the action before it ferments into trouble.

Rule-of-thumb: wines use about two-and-a-half pounds of

sugar to one gallon of juice. My grandparents used between one-half to one pound of sugar per gallon of water in making malt beers. I use one pound of sugar per gallon of water in making mock beers. I use one pound of sugar to five quarts of water in making soft beers.

Of course, there are as many variations of rule-of-thumb as there are brewers. I prefer my beer weak, my coffee and men strong, I tell Lewis, who is chief of sarsaparilla in our house.

In addition to water, yeast and sugar, homemade soft drinks entail flavoring agents such as ginger, oil of spruce, sassafras, birch extracts, cherries or, as my grandfather would say, "anything to give it character." Our friend Bill Crooks created a bottled beverage he called Horsetail. I don't know about the horse, but the tail had character; he used vanilla beans and peppercorns for flavoring.

Utensils for modern-day home brewing need not be elaborate. These are our basics: a polyethelene bucket and a ten-gallon plastic trash can or crock in which to make the brew; an unchipped enamel pot for recipes requiring boiling liquid; a siphon hose and a bench to put the brewing crock on to facilitate siphoning; cloths for straining; bottles, caps and a capper.

Some techniques call for the use of a hydrometer, thermometer and a simple immersion heater for accurate handling of home-brewed beverages. A hydrometer is not a mysterious, complicated tool; it merely measures the specific gravity of a liquid. Most water registers 1.000 (sometimes written 1 or 1000) on a hydrometer. Water mixed with a heavier substance registers heavier; hence water with extract and sugar would register heavier than 1.000, possibly 1.070 or 1.050. In fizzy bottled beverages, the yeast eats the sugar and replaces it with gas and alcohol; thus, as the sugar is used up, the register number will become lower; it will drop down closer to the gravity reading for plain water. Light beers with fizz are bottled and capped tightly to stop further yeast/sugar action when the hydrometer reads 1.005. This reading means that there is still a little unconverted sugar to produce sparkle when the bottle is opened. If a beverage goes "dead" or "flat," the sugar is used up.

A table using hydrometer readings has been worked out to explain how much alcohol by volume will be produced from the sugar content in a liquid. For example, if a hydrometer inserted in the beverage when it is first made floats upright and reads

1.035, the table would project that reading to about 3 percent alcohol by volume in the finished product. Tables are worked out in absolutes, purely specific gravity to alcohol content. But in home brewing, temperature, extracts, yeasts and other ingredients are likely to vary, so the hydrometer reading is merely an indicator of potential alcohol content.

Hydrometer Reading			*Alcohol Content by Volume*		
1.080	(when		11 percent	(probable	
1.070	first		9.2	end	
1.060		mixed	7.6		product)
1.050		in	6.0		
1.040		crock)	4.6		
1.030			2.9		
1.020			1.3		

Some home brewers add greater amounts of sugar to increase the alcohol potential of their brew. However, alcohol usually kills yeasts at about 14 percent (by volume), so increasing sugar after that potential percent is reached merely results in sweetening the brew. Heavily sugared home brews may sound great, but they may also make the inside of your skull sound like a sternwheeler backing off a sandbar.

Again, using a very shaky rule-of-thumb, about one-quarter cup of sugar raises the specific gravity reading on a hydrometer about five degrees.

For wine and other recipes which call for the fermentation of fruits, a gadget called a fermentation lock is helpful. This device keeps the brew free from bad yeasts (those yeasts that cause a sociopathic product) and keeps out air so that the good yeasts will utilize the sugar in the beverage to produce their own oxygen. Fermentation locks may be purchased at "home brew outfitters," but my grandfather made his locks by capping each gallon jar of fermenting liquid with a cork into which he had drilled a hole and inserted a short length of copper pipe. The protruding end of the pipe, which was about the size of my little finger, was connected to a small hose, and the far end of the hose was submerged in a glass of water. Thus, gases, carbon dioxide given off by the fermenting fruit, could bubble out of the gallon jar, but no air or bad yeasts could get into it. This process is called bubbling off because the glass of water that held the hose bubbled and burped with the gases from the brew.

One slightly alcoholic drink that utilized Granddaddy's cork and tubing fermentation lock was called berry water. It is easy to make, full-flavored, wine-like and may be made with any surplus berries: blackberries, June berries, strawberries, mulberries, blueberries and even gooseberries. Crush two-and-one-half pounds of berries together with one-and-one-half pounds of sugar, add one cup of cold water and press through a very fine jelly sack or cloth. Put the liquid into a gallon jar and add three quarts of tepid water and one-quarter teaspoon of dry yeast that has been dissolved with a little sugar in one-quarter cup of warm water. Mix in the juice of two lemons and "bubble off" or allow the berry water to ferment under a fermentation lock for two to four weeks.

When the action stopped, Granddaddy siphoned the liquid into sterilized heavy quart bottles and tied down the corks. His berry water was not aged, it was served icy cold as a pick-me-up during hot weather.

Berry water is a sprightly beverage but it is not a true fizzy drink. Mock beers and naturally carbonated "pops" are generally flavored with extracts, briefly fermented, then bottled and capped.

My grandfather made a spruce beer that was a typical example of his "from scratch" soft-beer-making methods. Spruce beer is made with an elixir of sassafras root (*Sassafras albidum*) and the twigs of black spruce (*Picea mariana*), an awkward, droopy-branched evergreen that grows on rocky slopes from Virginia northward.

For spruce beer my grandfather half-filled the canning kettle with water, brought it to a boil, and added a grocery sack full of washed black spruce twigs. He stirred them, brought the liquid to a boil, then dragged the kettle to the back of the stove and let the spruce steep. When it was lukewarm, he picked out the greenery, settled the spruce juice and strained it through a cloth laid across a ten-gallon crock. Next, he added four or five pounds of sugar, a cup of strong sassafras root elixir (made by simmering dried or fresh root overnight) and a package of yeast which had been dissolved with a teaspoon of sugar in a cup of water. He stirred the liquid, added water to make five gallons of beer, and covered it with a cloth. The spruce beer was allowed to ferment for about five days or a week. Fermentation takes less time during warm weather, but Granddaddy said that 70° to 80° F. is the most reliable fermentation temperature.

Granddaddy allowed the spruce beer to go "flat," that is, to return close to the 1.000 reading on a hydrometer, or just to lie dead or flat with no fermenting activity if he used the eyeball method; then he siphoned it into sterilized bottles.

The fermenting crock was kept on a low bench, the bottles lined up on the floor nearby, and the elevation drop from crock to bottles encouraged a fast siphon flow. Fill the bottles to within one-half inch from the top, Granddaddy said, and add one-quarter teaspoon of sugar to each quart. The added sugar primed the beer and gave sparkle to the drink. Each bottle was tightly capped and wired before being stored. Granddaddy allowed spruce beer to mature in a protected place at least three weeks before he chilled and served it.

My grandfather's spruce beers were different each time he made them because, he said, during some seasons spruce twigs hold more oils. Trees vary in oil content, too.

Our brewmeister neighbor brews a spruce beer using drug-store flavoring, and it is consistently good.

Put a three-pound can of light malt extract, three pounds of sugar and two quarts of water into a large enamel pot and simmer for ten minutes. Stir frequently. Add six tablespoons of food-grade oil of spruce and the juice of three lemons and pour everything into the crock. Add enough warm water to make five gallons, and mix in one-half package (or one level teaspoon) of dry yeast that has been dissolved with one teaspoon of sugar in one cup of warm water. Cover and allow the spruce beer to work for one week or until the fermentation has slowed but the beer has not stopped brewing. If you look carefully at the liquid surface tension in a streak of light you will be able to see pinpricks of activity, and the hydrometer reading will be between 1.005 and 1.003. Bottle spruce beer in heavy, sterilized bottles, cap tightly and store upright in a protected area for about six weeks before chilling and serving.

We sat in our neighbor's back yard one evening and ate corn on the cob and drank spruce beer. Lightning flashes lit the horizon, then suddenly it rained. Running to shelter, someone dropped his beer, and the essence of spruce rose from the deck where we gathered. For a moment earthly spruce odors carried me back to southeastern Alaska—rain forests rose up stoically through the valley mists, Indian campfires lit a protected shoreline, and tiny deer fed noiselessly in the indigo twilight—spruce beer does magical things to the senses.

Ginger beer is a happy change for muggy hot days. Make it two or three weeks before the dog days because ginger seems to become more spirited with age. I had a grand-uncle like that; he went out in a flash of glory. The older he became, the less he wanted to see, so the faster he drove—until he rammed and ignited a sulphur pile in Florida. I am convinced he never knew what he hit.

For ginger beer, dissolve a scant teaspoon of dried yeast with a teaspoon of sugar in a cup of warm water and set it aside to activate. Put seven-and-one-eighths cups of sugar together with two cups of lemon juice (natural or reconstituted) into a crock and cover with six quarts of boiling water. Stir and add three-and-one-half gallons (fourteen quarts) of cold water. For flavoring, mix three-and-one-half tablespoons each of ground ginger and cream of tartar, gradually add a little warm water and stir until the ginger and tartar are more or less in solution. (Powdered ginger will not dissolve, but there is nothing like lumpy ginger beer to set your teeth on edge so I try to mix it well.) Add the liquid ginger and tartar to the crock together with the activated yeast, stir well and bottle immediately in sterilized, strong, returnable-type bottles. Cap securely and lay the bottles on their sides for four days in a cool place. Store the bottles upright in a darkened, well-protected area and thoroughly chill before attempting to open them. This is a tricky brew. I have a notion that the song about "hot ginger and dynamite" was inspired by this fine drink.

Ginger beer, like other naturally carbonated bottled beverages, should be treated with respect. Exploding bottles can be highly dangerous. Rules to minimize accidents include:

Use a bit less yeast in warm weather.

Use heavy-duty bottles and fill bottles to within one-half inch from the top.

Barricade the storage area.

Store in a cool place.

Do not open any carbonated drink while it is warm. Chill thoroughly and open over a sink. Also, as my grandfather would advise, have a pitcher ready to catch the beer as it dances off the ceiling.

Sarsaparilla, the soothsayer's potent herbal cure for carbuncles and colds, has long been brewed into summer beverages. True sarsaparilla comes from Central and South America, a bramble of the smilax family, but its false cousin, wild sarsaparilla (*Aralia nudicaulis*), is common in temperate North American woodlands. Wild or false sarsaparilla sprouts from a horizontal root into a solitary, smooth-skinned leaf stalk which grows twelve to eighteen inches tall. The single-stemmed compound leaf has three divisions about six or eight inches above its root and each of its three divisions has three to five sharp-toothed, oval leaflets. Wild sarsaparilla leaves are reddish in May before the plant flowers. The naked flowering stalk grows from the foot close to but separate from the leaf stalk, and is shorter, as if it is shy and wants to hide beneath its leaf. Tiny white flowers bloom in June-July and produce clusters of dark berries each fall for juncos to feast upon when they migrate from the North. The slender, fragrant roots may be dug after the berries are mature and used fresh or dried for sarsaparilla drinks.

Homemade sarsaparilla of my grandparents' day was a low-alcohol drink that was popular with teetotalers, drinkers and children.

Wash and chop finely one quart of wild sarsaparilla root, or a mixture of sarsaparilla, American spikenard (*Aralia racemosa*) and sassafras roots. Cover with boiling water and simmer overnight in a lidded pot. Cool, strain, and strain a second time through a cloth into a large crock or plastic trash can. (Save the roots and reboil them for a milder sarsaparilla tea. They may be used over and over as long as the flavor lasts.) To the trash can or crock add four pounds of sugar and four tablespoons of imitation vanilla flavoring if sarsaparilla root extract is used alone. Mix in one gallon of warm water and stir well. Add a scant teaspoon of dry yeast dissolved with one teaspoon of sugar in a cup of warm water, fill the crock with warm water to make five gallons of liquid, stir and let stand for two hours. Siphon beverage into strong, returnable-type, sterilized quart bottles, cap tightly, and lay the bottles on their sides in room temperature (72° F.) for four days. Then very carefully move the bottles to a cool, darkened area, stand them upright, and leave them to mature and clear for about a week. Insure that the storage area is well protected with screening or cardboard boxes. Chill thoroughly before drinking.

Whether it is brewed by itself or with spikenard and sassafras root, sarsaparilla is a unique drink. My grandparents used to make it in stone gallon jars and wire down the caps. For the summer Sunday afternoon church socials, Granddaddy would gingerly transport the gallon jars in the back seat of the Essex to the churchyard, where the jars were put into washtubs of chipped ice. For fifteen cents you could buy a beer mug of sarsaparilla, sip some to make room, then inch your way up to the ice cream table and beg a scoop of ice cream to pop into it.

For the laying-bottles-on-their-sides step, I enclose six or eight quarts of immature soft beers in cardboard boxes. This precludes the danger of flying glass, but it does not do much holding of liquid if the caps are not tight. One year when our capper was on its last legs, a batch of bottle caps tilted and brew leaked through the porch flooring and dripped into the dogs' run below. That afternoon the dogs came into the kitchen hiccuping and smelling of brew. I thought the little thieves had learned to open bottles. When I investigated, I found that they had been downstairs catching the drip.

A fizz drink called gill ale was a popular malt beer enjoyed years ago by ladies who "didn't drink." I have tasted it and, personally, I'd rather drink. In some European countries at one time, gill ale was highly popular; even its name, derived from the Old French *guiller*, means to ferment or make merry. Now the poor little gill plant has trailed its persistent way into lawns and pastures, where it is despised by suburbanites and hated by cattle. Ground ivy, gill-over-the-ground (*Glecoma hederacea* or *Nepeta glechoma*), is the mint used in gill ale.

Wash and boil one pint of fresh or dried ground ivy leaves in a pint of water for fifteen minutes. Strain into a crock, add four-and-a-half-pounds of sugar, a half-dozen thinly sliced lemons (including peels), one three-pound can of light malt and two gallons of warm water. Mix well. Add one package of dry yeast which has been dissolved with one teaspoon sugar in a cup of warm water. Fill the crock with warm water to make eight or ten gallons of liquid. Cover and allow to ferment at room temperature, 72° F., for five to seven days.

When the hydrometer reads 1.005, or the brew lies almost flat, gill ale may be bottled in sterilized bottles, and capped tightly. They should be stored upright in a cool, dark place for six weeks before chilling and opening. This is a heady, sparkling drink, but I think it tastes terrible.

"Mock Hops" is more attractive to my untrained taste buds. Boil a cupful of dried hops (available at some drugstores) in a pint of water for fifteen minutes. Strain through a cloth into a crock or plastic trash can. (My grandfather poured the liquid, hops and all, into the crock, then strained it as he siphoned the brew.) Add four pounds of sugar, a three-pound can of dark malt extract, about two gallons of warm water, and stir until all is dissolved. Pour in one cup of warm water in which a package of yeast and a teaspoon of sugar have been dissolved, and fill the crock with warm water to make ten gallons. Cover your Mock Hops and allow it to ferment for about a week. I start testing my light beers after about five days. I watch the surface tension of the crock for slowdown and I poke in the hydrometer. When the reading is 1.005 (or when the liquid lies still and heavy), siphon into sterilized quart bottles and cap tightly. Allow three to six weeks for Mock Hops to mature. This full-bodied, mildly alcoholic brew is a drink that grows on you. At first taste it seems malty and bitter, but after the glass is half finished you wonder if you'll ever go back to the pallid "kid stuff" again.

Gorse, molasses beer, licorice beer, birch beer: our forefathers brought many mock, lightly alcoholic beer recipes from the old countries. Recipes were changed to fit the materials at hand and new concoctions were brewed.

My grandmother made a mildly fermented honey drink with dandelions. She called it Gorse. Now I know that there is a European evergreen shrub with yellow blossoms called gorse or furze, but when I was young I thought Gorse was the name of a beverage, like Coke.

In May, Grandma would send me into the yard to pick a quart of dandelion petals. That's a lot of petals, but fortunately she told me not to pack them. She warned that any green from the plant and the dandelion milk would make the Gorse bitter, so plucking yellow centers only, I crawled in the grass and studied the earth and its awakening bug population.

Grandma mixed about five cups of honey with five quarts of water and boiled it for three minutes, then poured the boiling liquid into the crock that contained one quart of dandelion petals. She stirred with a wooden spoon, adding two sliced lemons and a cup of Chinese tea, then mashed the petals and lemons as she "worked" her Gorse. When the brew had cooled to luke-warm she mixed in a teaspoon of yeast that had been dissolved with a teaspoon of sugar in a cup of warm water, then dropped the whites of two eggs into the crock and added water to make two-and-one-half gallons. Grandma covered her Gorse and left it to ferment for a week, or until the hydrometer reading was between 1.005 and 1.000. She said that Gorse should be bottled when "its spirit was at peace."

Grandma strained the peaceful liquid, let it "settle out the clouds," siphoned it into heavy, sterilized bottles and capped them tightly. Gorse should be stored upright in a cool, dark place for a month or two before being put into the icebox. Always chill before opening. I remember one bottle that sprayed foam like a fire extinguisher when it was uncapped at room temperature.

A mellow, tawny, tingling drink, my grandmother's Gorse was great.

Molasses beer is rum-like and hearty. My grandfather used to heat one gallon of water to boiling and slowly add one gallon of molasses together with a three-pound can of malt extract. The gooey liquid was stirred and just as the boiling point was reached, one pint of fresh female, virgin-type hop flowers (*Humulus lupulus*) was stirred in. The kettle was moved to the back of the cook stove and allowed to cool, or "gather body" as my grandfather called the process.

A cake of yeast and one teaspoon of sugar were dissolved in one cup of warm water and added to the molasses liquid as soon as it was lukewarm. My grandfather poured the molasses beer into a ten-gallon crock and stirred as the crock was filled with tepid water. Sometimes he added a bit of bitters (wormwood tea, *Artemisia absinthum*, infused in a cup of boiling water) to cut the rummy flavor. Then he covered the crock to allow the mixture to ferment in privacy. The crock almost seemed to quake with the ferment, brown scum and hops leaves rose up and molasses solids sank and rose again, then suddenly all was quiet and a sweet liquor was born.

Molasses beer must work at least seven days in a covered container at about 72° F., and my grandfather advised that this beer be allowed to "go dead." The hydrometer reading should be very close to 1.000 before the beer is bottled in heavy, sterilized containers and capped tightly. Molasses, like honey, often contains unknown sugars that are prone to stimulate yeasts in the bottle, produce gas and POW! Because of uncertain sugar content, molasses beer should be allowed to ferment until the yeasts are inactive, and it should be bottled in heavy-duty bottles.

Though reminiscent of rum, molasses beer is not heavily alcoholic. If you do not care for its strong character, open the bottles, let them set and the liquid will turn into a fine sour malt vinegar that is excellent as a marinade for meat or fowl.

I often roast meat of questionable age or tenderness in a quart of sour beer (molasses or hops, not licorice or root beers). I simply salt, pepper and flour robust cuts of beef or pork, place the meat in a roasting pan and pour one quart of sour beer over it. I cover the pan and slow-roast, 325° F., thirty to forty-five minutes to the pound. I add a little water if the beer marinade boils dry. With chuck or tough beef, I pop in potatoes, carrots and an onion or two, one hour before dinner. For fresh pork roast, I pour off excess fat, add potatoes, carrots, onion, two cups of tomatoes and one-half teaspoon of Italian seasoning, one hour before serving. Ten minutes before blastoff, I drop in wedges of cabbage. This makes a superb one-dish—all man—meal.

I am not a fancy cook. When I learned one day that we were having a connoisseur of good food, an outspoken elderly aunt, as a guest, I shuddered, then decided to serve just what we were going to have anyway: pork in sour beer, avocado salad, light bread roll and squash pie. It turned out to be an excellent dinner. Beer flavors, colors, glazes and delivers the *coup de maître* to the tonsils.

I have poured a quart of sour beer over a leg of lamb and slow-roasted the meat in a covered pan. I poured off the fat and served the juice without thickening as a provocative sauce for steamed rice. I once marinated a nineteen-pound chicken-yard-run turkey in sour beer, then basted it with about a pint of the liquid. That day I had to barricade the kitchen door to keep my excited household from descending upon the fowl before it was done. Sour beer cooked with meat stimulates every active olfactory gland for blocks around.

Bad beer seems to repent its sourness when used in cooking; as a marinade, sour beer seems to rise up and permeate all it touches with goodness. For that reason I rarely throw out undrinkable brew.

Licorice beer is an oldie. My grandfather put one pound of licorice hard candy and three pinches of hop flowers (both purchased at the drugstore) into a gauze bag and gently boiled them in two quarts of water for thirty minutes. Hop flowers look like small bunches of green leaves and they secrete resins which flavor and feed yeast brews.

When the licorice-and-hops liquid had cooled to lukewarm, he poured it into a crock with a bucketful of warm water and added a three-pound can of dark malt extract, four pounds of sugar and a package of yeast dissolved with a teaspoon of sugar in a cup of warm water. The crock was stirred thoroughly and then filled with warm water to make about ten gallons. He covered the brew and allowed it to work and ferment at 72° F. for five days, or until the beer was almost dead. If he used the hydrometer, when the reading was 1.005, he bottled it in heavy, pre-boiled bottles, and he capped each bottle tightly. My grandfather let licorice beer age six weeks, or until Uncle Otto, Grandma's brother, came to visit; then the two of them would work on the batch together.

Ten gallons of beer usually cans into thirty-five quarts because the siphon hose should not lie on the bottom of the beer crock, nor should it be allowed to pick up sediment. Yeast and malt sediment clouds beer. Granddaddy devised a weight which he tied to one end of the siphon hose so that the hose would float about four inches above the bottom of the crock. The other end of the siphon hose was changed from bottle to bottle as each was filled with the siphoned fluid. Most bottled home-brewed products contain a film of sediment, and should be decanted carefully into a pitcher before pouring into glasses in order to leave the murky liquid in the bottom of the bottle.

Birch beer stirs my memories. Although I have heard stories that it is highly alcoholic, Grandma made birch beer for the neighborhood youngsters. I remember playing Hide and Seek on nights of sticky, sweaty, itchy heat. Finally, we'd all call "King's X" and crowd Grandma's back porch for birch beer. Its wintergreen coolness was like a fresh breeze. Most young people like it as well as they do root beer.

Pour one gallon of boiling water over three-and-three-fourths teaspoons of oil of wintergreen. (Be sure that the wintergreen

extract you buy from the druggist is for internal use. The wintergreen you buy for earache drops holds little merit for beer,
unless you wish to poison your children.) Add four gallons of
cold water, three pounds of sugar and a scant teaspoon of dry
yeast which has been dissolved with a teaspoon of sugar in a cup
of warm water. Stir well, cover and let stand for two hours. Siphon into strong, sterilized bottles, cap tightly and lay the bottles on their sides at 72° F. for four days. Then store in a well-
protected, darkened, cool area. Chill thoroughly before opening.
On a hot night, with heaps of plain sugar cookies, there is no
finer treat for a mob of rollicking thirteen-year-olds.

I have heard that fizzy homemade "soda pop" may be made
by dissolving one-quarter teaspoon of bicarbonate of soda and
one tablespoon of sugar in one cup of water, then adding two or
three tablespoons of lemon juice. The liquid fizzes hilariously,
and if you can, you should drink it immediately. Unfortunately,
when I was young one of Grandmother's favorite remedies for
fever was baking soda dissolved in water taken internally. I
used to hold my nose, shiver and swallow. Then Grandma would
place a cold silver knife under my chin to keep me from throw-
ing up. The cold knife inhibits vomiting all right, but the soda
treatment also inhibited my tolerance for "soda pop."

Lively Lemonade, Cherry Bounce and Currant Crush, although not "pop" or fizz beverages, are mildly alcoholic and
fun drinks for summer.

For a lemonade treat, roll and slice six lemons, paper thin.
Layer the slices in a pitcher with two tablespoons of granulated
sugar for each lemon. Put a tray of ice cubes (without the tray)
on top of the sugared lemons and let stand for an hour or two.
When ready to serve, stir with a long spoon for a minute, trying
not to mash the slices, then pour in two bottles of ginger ale and
one bottle of port wine. A cheery counterfeit, Lively Lemonade
makes a pretty, fizzy drink, which I serve with a straw. I also let
a few limp lemon slices fall into each glass to be nibbled as a
thirst quencher.

Grandma's Cherry Bounce used to be made when birds gathered for their annual reunion and tart, pie cherries hung plump
and red on the trees. From the first crack of dawn, you could
hear chirpy family arguments, catbird bickerings and loud-
mouthed insults flung by the jays. One cherry tree was next
to my bedroom window where I could hear the birds scream at

each other and watch them gorge themselves until their craws were so heavy they could barely take off.

I didn't like to pick cherries but I like pies, so it didn't take much intellect to figure out what to do if I expected pie.

For Grandma's Cherry Bounce, first beat the birds to the cherries, then beat the cherries to a pulp. In a large crock, mix five pounds of pitted sweet, tart or wild cherries with two-and-a-half pounds of sugar, cover and set the crock in the cellar for two days. Add a quart of cheap vodka, stir, cover securely and let stand in a cool, dark place for six weeks. Stir the fruit from time to time, and taste the juice to test its developing character. When your eyes water and flavor explodes in your mouth, you know the cherries have given their all to Grandma's Bounce. Strain through two cloths, and if there is any left, bottle in sterilized bottles and seal.

For a crimson cordial, use your best glasses and pour this royal liquor over crushed ice. As a peppy party punch, gradually add one quart of chilled Cherry Bounce to two or three quarts of icy ginger ale and serve in goblets. Fizz bubbles will perk the liquid and exquisite cherry red lights will do wild dances in the crystal juice.

Currant Crush. Take five pounds of currants, pick off stems and shake out bugs, crush the fruit with four pounds of sugar in a crock and cover with four gallons of boiling water. When lukewarm add one cake of yeast dissolved with one teaspoon of sugar in a cup of warm water. Cover the crock and allow the crush to ferment at 72° F. for a week. Strain through two thicknesses of cloth, rinse the crock, and return the liquid to ferment for another week. If you use a hydrometer, take readings, and when 1.003 or 1.002 is reached, bottle in heavy, dark glass bottles and cap securely.

If you use the eyeball method, wait until the brownish liquor is nearly "dead," that is, until few bubbles are seen in the surface tension of the crush. Siphon into sterilized bottles and cap tightly. Amber, fizzy Currant Crush shows mature promise in three weeks, but like proper wine and women, "a little age on them makes them better."

Fizzy bottled beverages are fun to explore. Care should be taken, however, to use only strong, returnable-type bottles for fermenting soft beers, and each bottle should be extremely cold before you open it. Bottles should be stored behind a screen or boxed to protect anyone close by in case a bottle builds up pressure and explodes.

There is no such thing as "carefree" home-brewed beverages. Fizzy drinks are exciting to make and to share, but as the proverb goes, "the wife of a careless brewmeister is almost a widow."

7

Pickle Power

"There are four kinds of power: money, force, prestige, and pickle," a colorfully tattooed cook in Alaska once told me. "Most people think that money runs the world, but it's pickle power that creates the action. Pickle power is the ferment of change." Though the cook appeared to have spent several years in the boxing ring (his nose had been pushed to one side and an ear was affixed to the wrong place on his massive neck), he spoke with fluidity and resolution. "Pickling and fermenting affect all living processes," he asserted. "Without ferment the earth would stagnate."

My cook acquaintance had learned about power through experience. Once a construction laborer, he had saved and bought out a nearly defunct but prestigious road-building firm. He had learned about payoffs and force, about state contracts and the power of prestige, and he had learned about money power when his wife skipped with his bank account. He finally resolved that pickle power was the most dependable. And every Saturday night he got drunk.

The cook was intimately familiar with all kinds of pickles: he brined or fermented every food that arrived on his remote Alaskan shore. He followed ancient time-consuming ways and the faster middle-American methods, and sometimes he pickled fruits in spiced vinegar.

Today the word pickle is more often associated with vinegar, but years ago pickling meant the preserving of foods in brine. A lactic acid fermentation often took place in the brine and the resultant sour, vinegar-like flavor was said to be "pickle."

In brining vegetables, osmosis takes place: the juices are drawn from the vegetables into the brine and the brine is absorbed by the vegetables. The liquids from the vegetables contain sugar that is converted into lactic acid by the lactic acid bacteria, causing fermentation, as in sauerkraut.

Utensils needed for brining and pickling vegetables are few, with small crocks, barrels or plastic buckets being the main needs. Because metal causes discoloration and an off-taste in some pickled foods, enamel or wooden spoons and enameled colanders and kettles should be used. Fitted covers for the crocks, weights, cheesecloth and paraffin are also necessary. Old-timers were said to have covered pickles with grape, beet or cabbage leaves which contributed to the ferment. My grandparents used leaves and paraffin-dipped wooden lids for their pickle barrels, but my grandfather was a cooper and could make lids. I use dinner plates.

Kitchen scales and a salinometer, an instrument for measuring the salt strength of brine, and a sugar hydrometer are sometimes required and are always useful in pickling.

Supplies for brining and pickling vary, but the main ingredient is salt. Common salt or coarse grades may be used, but salt with additives, such as iodine, is not recommended.

Clear, forty- to sixty-grain-strength vinegar (4 to 6 percent acetic acid) is required in making sour, sweet or dill-flavored pickles. Distilled and white vinegar is sometimes called for.

Granulated sugar is used in sweet pickle recipes and to soften the harshness in some sour pickles.

Spices are usually required for sweet and mixed pickled vegetables. Mixed whole spices may be purchased or peppers (black and cayenne), cloves, celery seed, cinnamon, caraway, cardamom, bay leaves, ginger, horseradish, coriander, mace and mustard may be mixed. Oil of spices is called for in some pickle recipes, but care should be taken that the oils are fresh because their essence is not as long-lasting as whole spices.

Dill is a special spice in that it may be grown in most parts of the United States and the entire herb may be used as well as dill seed. Dill herb should be cut when the seeds are mature but before they shatter, and dill may be used green, dried or brined. My grandmother brined a quart or so of dill each year by packing the mature green dill heads and herb in one quart of water into which one cup of salt had been dissolved. Tightly covered, brined dill kept for a long time and she often used a little dill brine for flavoring in salads and sauces. In recipes calling for dried dill, double the amount of brined or fresh dill is used.

Various types of brine are made from different proportions of salt to water. The amount of liquid needed for brining vegetables is about one-half the volume of the material to be fermented. For example, if five gallons of vegetables are to be brined, two-and-one-half gallons of brine is required. The three most common brines used in pickling foods are 5, 10 and 15 percent. Five percent brine, made by dissolving three-quarters of a cup of salt in approximately one gallon of water, is used for firming some vegetables. It permits rapid fermentation, but produce kept in 5 percent brine will spoil unless processed further, preserved in vinegar, or vacuum sealed. A 10 percent brine is made by dissolving one-and-one-half cups of salt in approximately one gallon of water and is used with vegetables that are to be fermented. The resultant mixture of brine and lactic acid will keep most vegetables, but the brine must be maintained at 10 percent strength. A 15 percent brine is made by dissolving two-and-a-quarter cups of salt in approximately one gallon of water and is used to store fermented vegetables because the stronger solution of salt checks fermentation. All containers of brined vegetables should be sealed with paraffin for long keeping.

Temperature should be maintained at 80° to 85° F. for fermentation of vegetables in brine, and 50° to 55° F. for storage.

Fermenting or pickling by the use of straight salt is most familiar in sauerkraut made from cabbage. My Alaskan friend krauted carrots, green beans, turnips and a local weed of the Polygonum family.

His carrot kraut was excellent when cooked with a chunk of smoked ham. Shred five pounds of carrots and sprinkle them with three-and-a-quarter tablespoons of salt, mix well and press into a crock. Press the shredded carrots and salt until a brine appears. The brine must cover the vegetables or they will spoil. Keep the carrot kraut in a warm place, about 80° F., and keep the kraut under the brine by using a plate and a weight. Cover with cheesecloth and a lid. Peek every so often to see that the brine has not evaporated (add 10 percent brine if it has), and skim any scum that forms because scum destroys the acidity of the top layer. When fermentation slows, in about two weeks, cook a batch of carrot kraut to taste it, then store it in a cool place or seal it. To seal kraut, pour melted paraffin over the weighted plate and dribble wax around the edges. If unsealed, carrot kraut should be eaten in six weeks.

To serve, wash the kraut, add water to cover, cook over a slow fire, and flavor with drippings or meat. Pickling or krauting carrots gives them personality, and their zippy taste, together with their tawny good looks, makes them irresistible.

Many American Indian tribes traditionally pickled in salt as a means of saving surplus foods. The Iroquois nations pickled corn that fermented into an acid brine. The Senecas pickled cherries and berries in a brine that changed into a heavy, holding vinegar. The Indians of the South are known to have preserved semi-dried beans and roots in salt, and fermentation changed the brine to an acid liquid. The Pima of Arizona preserved watermelons by burying them in the sands of the river bed and called this "pickling." Berries were fermented into a pickle mush by the Northwest Indians, and sub-Arctic natives have long pickled greens in brine to form a sauerkraut. I can find no reference to the ancient Sioux pickling foods, but this omission in their diet may have had roots in the cult belief that an individual would develop characteristics of the food he consumed. If a Sioux relished rabbit, it was believed his ears would grow or perhaps he would acquire a bunny tail. If a Sioux overate of turtle flesh, it was thought that he would become lazy. An expectant mother would not dare to eat pig lest her child have small eyes.

The Tsimshians of southeastern Alaska tell the story of a beautiful princess, the daughter of a great chief, who refused to marry her cousin as her father wished. Defiant, she canoed away from her village and hid in a cove, where she lived on fern roots which she preserved by salting them to create a pickle. One morning a young Indian came to her camp. The princess was glad to have company and when, after several weeks, he asked her to become his wife and go home with him, she said yes. The young man gathered up all of her pickled fern roots, put them into his canoe and spread mats of cedar bark

over them as a bed for the princess. At high tide they pad-
dled away. Soon the princess became tired and lay down. When
she awoke, she was in a large house surrounded by many people. She became frightened and ran back to the canoe, but when
she came to the shore the canoe was gone. There was only a
drift log. Bewildered, she returned to the house to seek her husband. In his place was an otter. Aghast, she ran from room to
room. She found only otters, and every otter was gobbling up
her pickled fern roots.

The otters kept her in their colony and made her dig roots
and pickle them. One day when the princess was on the beach,
an old otter slid down the bank and said, "Give me root!" but
the girl cried that she was about to give birth to a child. Then
all the otter clan gathered and shouted, "Cast this woman out!
Turn her out!" and the princess was thrown into a canoe and
pushed into the water. In the bottom of the boat she found some
pickled fern roots, which she chewed on while Little Otter was
born.

Shortly after his birth, Little Otter slithered from the canoe.
The princess lay in the canoe and cried for three days because
her child had left her. Then she heard singing, and when she
sat up she saw her father. He took her home and she obediently
married her cousin, but she never again pickled fern roots, nor
did she bear a child.

The Indian woman from an inlet near Metlakatla who told
me this story shyly confided that ever since then her tribe has
believed that pickled fern roots cause sterility. She repeated this
with a twinkle in her eye as she fed her eight children; then she,
her husband and I sat down to eat a meal of spring salmon and
fern roots. Actually, the pickled roots, which looked like mini-
turnips, were very good. I asked the Metlakatlan lady how she
prepared them. She told me that every year her family gathered
fern roots, pickled them in salt and sealed their containers with
a mixture of one-third resin and two-thirds beeswax. This sealing mix was heated, stirred, allowed to cool somewhat, then
pressed with a hot knife across the top and around the sides of
her lidded storage jar. I could not identify the fern roots which
she said were sometimes steamed and eaten fresh as well as
being preserved in salt or, as she called the preserving process,
pickled. The root probably fermented.

Pickled Alaskan fern roots reminded me of the home-grown

olives brined by friends in California. Both utilized time-honored methods of preserving, both foods were drenched in tangy, sour-sweet goodness, and I found it impossible to stop nibbling on either delicacy. Our former neighbors hand-picked their olives because they said shaking injures the fruit as well as the trees.

For each pound of green but mature olives, they mixed a pound of hardwood ashes and an ounce of slaked lime with enough water to form a soft paste. Then they stirred in the olives. The cement-like mass of olives and wet ashes was covered with a layer of dry ashes and left to "extract." By that, they meant to extract bitumen, which they knew had been "extracted" when the stones could be readily slipped out of the olive by squeezing. The length of time for the bitumen to be extracted varies from two hours to two days. The variance, they told me, is due to differences in olive ripeness and the quality of ashes and lime.

As soon as the bitterness was extracted and the pits came free easily, the olives were washed and soaked in fresh water, which was either run through the container or changed every hour for twenty-four hours. When the water ceased to be discolored and no longer tasted "ashy," the olives were put into jars and covered with a brine made of one cup of salt to one quart of water. Our friends sealed their crocks of brined olives with several layers of paraffin and stored them in a dark, cool, dry place. The brine will keep the olives for years without spoiling, but for best results, the brine should be changed several times each year.

Our neighbors kept their green olives in one-gallon crocks for at least six weeks before they ate them. The crocks were not re-sealed, nor did they further flavor the olives with red peppers, coriander, garlic or cloves as some people did. Their plain olives were intensely nutty in flavor, juicy and fully satisfying.

Although I did not taste them, our olive friends said that sometimes they took the brine-cured olives, pitted them and inserted a caper, a bit of anchovy or a tidbit of pickled mushroom into the seed hole. They put the fancy olives into small containers, covered them with olive oil, lidded them tightly and stored them until needed.

As an experiment our friends extracted oil from full ripe olives by heaping the freshly gathered fruit into a colander and allowing the oil to be pressed out by the weight of the olives. "Virgin oil," they called the clear golden liquid.

They also tried putting the dripping pulp which remained after the oil had been extracted into a sack and gently squeezing it. This was called "cooking oil."

The squeezed-out pulp was then dumped into a kettle of water and boiled and skimmed. This oil they gave away to a ranch for use as a leather preservative, and they told us that commercial houses utilize such oil for soap.

In olden days, the olive stones were broken after boiling and skimming, the mushy pulp was boiled and skimmed a second time, and the inferior, off-colored oil was burned in lamps. The final pulp of the olives was pressed into cakes, dried and burned as fuel, and the ashes formed a potash fertilizer that was spread under olive trees.

Our friends did not keep their homemade olive oil unsealed for any length of time because, they told us, natural oil is like wine. Unsealed it spoils.

After the olives have been pickled for two or three months, some people store them in olive oil. To do this, they select the largest olives, prick each one with a needle, and place them in half-gallon jars. They sprinkle dried garlic, cloves, red chilies (dried) or rosemary twigs on top of the olives and cover them with olive oil. Lidded tightly, they will keep for a long time.

Most old recipes for cucumber pickles called for the straight brining of cucumbers to firm and preserve them. My grandmother said that fruit should be under brine no later than twenty-four hours after it had been picked. She salted nearly all her cucumbers before making them into sour, sweet or dills.

To make fermented cucumber pickles, cut unbruised, nearly ripe fruit with one-quarter inch of the stems intact. Because of the high water content of cucumbers, the brine for medium-sized cucumbers should be strong at the beginning of the fermentation period and replacement salt should be added gradually over a period of several weeks. Active fermentation usually continues for ten to thirty days (if the temperatures remain between 80° and 85° F.) because the sugar withdrawn from the friut is used as food by the brine bacteria. Too much salt added after fermentation is under way reduces the bacterial action and less acid is formed; thus fermentation is retarded. If you don't want retarded pickles, brine at a leisurely pace. "Go slow," my grandmother would emphasize after she lectured on the beauties of a "gifted pickle." I repeat her words and directions to myself when I pickle, but I was born a swifty, so my pickles usually end up retarded.

For small quantities of fermented pickles, my grandmother packed twelve pounds of uniform-size cucumbers in a four-gallon crock and added six quarts of 10 percent brine. (That works out to approximately one-fourth bushel of cucumbers and two-and-one-fourth cups of salt dissolved in six quarts of water.) She covered the pickles with a cloth and a weighted wooden lid that fit inside the crock.

Early the next day, she added two-and-one-fourth cups more salt by placing the dry salt on the lid which was submerged in brine. The salt gradually dissolved and wept into the brine. If you added salt directly to the brine, she said, it would sink and the salt solution at the bottom would be strong while the top cucumbers would spoil. "Cucumbers should be kept under brine at all times," Grandmother insisted, "and if scum forms, skim it off or it will retard your pickles."

At the end of the first week, and at the end of every week for five weeks straight, she put eight tablespoons of salt on the lid. The salt gradually sank and by the time the next week's salting day rolled around it had dissolved. If any wild yeasts or molds had formed on the surface, she removed it by skimming.

About six weeks after the cucumbers are first put into brine they are cured. Cured cucumbers are firm, somewhat translucent, and dark to olive green in color. If any cucumbers are whiteys or floaters, if they are shriveled or slippery, they are definitely disadvantaged citizens of the pickle barrel and should be removed. Do not despair, however; they can be rehabilitated and become contributing citizens of relishes or mixed pickles. After the rejects are sorted, the cured pickles may be covered with a 15 percent holding brine (two-and-one-quarter cups of salt dissolved in one gallon of water), lidded, and a layer of hot paraffin poured over the exposed surface around the weighted cover.

In addition to curing vegetables, krauts, olives and cucumbers in straight salt or brine, some people pickle, that is, flavor and preserve food, by the use of two processes. First they brine the produce to save it during the rush of harvest; next they draw out some of the salt and further process the vegetables in spiced vinegar. My grandmother's barrels of cucumbers that she cured in brine were usually further processed into sour, sweet, dill or mixed pickles at a later date, when garden canning was "slacking off."

Brine-cured pickles must receive a processing in water to remove the excess of salt. If they are to be used as salt pickles, only a brief leaching is required, but if they are going to be made into sours or sweets, most, but not all, of the salt should be removed.

To leach or remove salt from cured cucumbers, place them in a large enamel vessel, cover with water and heat slowly to about 120° F.; hold at that temperature, stirring frequently for about ten to twelve hours. Grandma used to put the pickles on the back of the stove overnight. She poured off the water and repeated the leaching until they had only a slightly salty taste. I used to like to nibble on salt pickles, and when I passed the stove I'd snitch one.

Grandma made sour pickles first because they were the easiest. I didn't like them, but that did not influence her. She drained about forty cured and leached four-inch cucumbers, put them into a gallon crock and covered them with forty- to fifty-grain vinegar. She lidded the crock with a weighted cover and put it in a cool, dark place. She replaced the original vinegar after a month or two because she said it would be diluted by the brine contained in the pickles. If they are kept covered with vinegar, lidded and weighted, sour pickles will stay crunchy and tart until eaten, she said. I did not taste them— sour pickles smelled too puckery for me.

Sweet pickles I liked. Cover the brined, leached and drained cucumbers with forty- to fifty-grain vinegar and let them stand for one week. Remember to lid and weight each crock. (I failed to do this one time and my cucumbers floated, swelled up and died.)

Discard the first vinegar and cover the pickles with one gallon of vinegar (forty- to fifty-grain) which has been simmered with one ounce of pickling spices (tied in a sack) and four pounds of sugar. Cover the crock with a weighted lid.

It is important, my grandmother told me, to keep the acidity of the liquid used on pickles as high as possible. Vinegar of less than thirty-grain strength permits wild yeasts to grow, and spoilage occurs. If more sugar is desired, it should be added gradually. Heating spices with vinegar improves the flavor, but too long a heating causes the vinegar to darken.

Sweet pickles may be held under the vinegar liquid until eaten or packed into sterilized bottles, covered with boiling liquid and sealed.

Brined and leached cucumbers may be made into dill pickles, mixed, sliced, spiced, mustard, or most other kinds of pickle happiness.

Grandmother held pickling to be one of the more pleasing pursuits of homemaking. She said that there were no urgencies or absolutes in pickling, that a woman could take her time and create beautiful things in a pickle barrel. She believed that pickling was a leisurely way to save the garden's goodness. Actually, her ideas of thrift and leisure could be cited as key concepts to living naturally with the land. The land itself is rarely in a hurry; it builds itself up, feeds itself, and moves from place to place in leisurely fashion. Only under the stress of storms and eruptions does land hurry; then it often devastates itself. Under natural conditions, land moves in a thrifty and leisurely manner, and for man to live in harmony with his land, thrift and leisurely interaction are essential.

I used to exchange pickle recipes with a pretzel vendor who had a wife, garden, pickling shed and mother-in-law across the state line. "I'm a dill man, myself," he told me. Later, I learned that he was also a bigamist. The IRS exposed his secret and he disappeared from both his pretzel route and his pickle shed.

The pretzel man's dills required about half as much preparation time as my grandmother's brined pickles. Fermentation is much more rapid in a weaker brine; the keeping qualities are weaker, too, he told me, but his dills were very good.

In a four-gallon crock, place a layer of grape leaves, a layer of dill, and one-half ounce of mixed pickling spice. Fill the crock to within three inches of the top with washed and uniform-size cucumbers. Sprinkle on another half-ounce of pickling spice and a layer of dill, then top with grape leaves. Dissolve one pound of salt in two gallons of cold water, mix in one pint of forty- to fifty-grain vinegar, and pour over the cucumbers. Cover with a weighted board to hold the pickles under the brine.

"Keep your pickles warm," my pretzel man advised. "Hot

brine kills fermentation and frigid dills don't work good, either," he warned. He also said he skimmed his dills every four or five days to guard against "promiscuous yeasts."

Fermentation is usually completed in two weeks, at which time the dill pickles may be eaten or canned to preserve them. To preserve dills, pack the cured pickles into sterilized quart jars together with a pinch of dill herb or seed. Add one-half cup of vinegar to each jar. Strain, boil and cool the brine from the crock and use it to finish filling the jars. Seal and store.

I make Swifty Chunks out of oddball cucumbers. This combines a brief brining process with a vinegar dip, and while they cannot compare with my grandmother's product, they are quick and edible.

I make a brine of one pound of salt dissolved in one gallon of cold water and soak a peck of whole cucumbers in it for three days. I throw the brine away and cover the cucumbers with clear water. Two days later I rinse them and cut them into chunks. Next I measure the pickles and for each quart of chunks I make a solution of one quart of vinegar, one teaspoon of powdered alum and two quarts of water. I soak my Swifty Chunks for two days in this solution and throw the liquid away. Now I am ready to really pickle my chunks.

I boil a pickling syrup of one-and-one-half-pints of vinegar, one pint of water, nine cups of sugar, one ounce of cinnamon sticks (crumbled), one teaspoon of mustard seed and one teaspoon of whole cloves. The odors that waft from the kitchen during this step whet everyone's appetite for pickle cheer, but I tell them to put the brakes on.

Pour the hot syrup over the pickles and let them stand overnight to drink in all that spicy delight. The next day I drain the syrup from the pickles, reheat it and pour it over them again. This process is repeated for three days, and on the fourth day we nibble, pack the chunks in hot jars and seal.

My Alaskan "pickle power" cook made a piccalilli out of odds and ends of vegetables left over from his restaurant. He combined the use of brine and spiced vinegar methods to create his piquant piccalilli. The cook filled gallon commercial mayonnaise jars with a salt brine "strong enough to float an egg," or one-and-one-half cups of salt to one gallon of water, then he cast in leftover produce: onions, mushroom bits, cauliflower and broccoli stems, fancy carrot shapes, sliced turnips, radish roses, green tomatoes, beans, celery, red pepper pods, strips of ginger, horseradish discs and any other "spare parts around the kitchen." In a week or two, when a couple of gallons of vegetables had been collected, he removed them from the brine, packed them into sterilized mayonnaise jars and poured a vinegar pickle over them. To make the pickle he boiled one gallon of vinegar and added eight tablespoons of salt, four tablespoons of ground ginger, two tablespoons each of pepper and allspice, then mashed two tablespoons each of mustard and tumeric into a paste and added it to the boiling vinegar. When all the spices were boiling and a sniff brought tears to your eyes, the cook covered the pot and removed it from the fire. After it cooled, he poured the spiced vinegar over the piccalilli to cover, lidded the jar and stored each jar in a cool place for six months.

That road-builder-turned-pickler had a brain full of pickled ideas. One time he begged me to bring him a bag of bell peppers on my return from the "South Forty-eight," so I hand-carried a shopping bag of sweet pepper beauties and stuffed it under my plane seat. I was also hand-carrying my rifle, two bulky gifts, an envelope of important papers, my overnight bag, hat and purse. Seated between two handsome men I soon forgot my peppers and it was not until I was enroute to my shuttle plane that I remembered them. Racing back to the airport I loped onto the field just as the steps were being rolled away. With frantic arm signals I persuaded the attendant to let me rescue my peppers. Then I proceeded to leave them on the second plane—a seaplane that flew me to my island home. Three days and many radio-telephone conversations later, I received the peppers from a fish cannery where they had been unloaded in error.

To pickle peppers, the cook laid several sprays of dill together with a handful of pickling spice in a beer keg and arranged the whole, washed peppers in layers, stems up, on top of the spice. He scattered more dill and sprinkled three handfuls of salt on the packed peppers. He boiled a gallon of vinegar with a gallon of water and a handful of pickling spice, cooled it and poured it over the peppers. The barrel of pickling peppers was topped with a weighted plate and a clean cloth and allowed to cure for three weeks in a cool pantry, then eaten with meats and salads, or stuffed and baked. My friends and I liked them scrambled with eggs for a Sunday night supper after a hard day of skiing on the virgin slopes above Sitka. Scrambled pickled peppers make a perfect ending to a day in God's heady highlands.

To pickle small, solid green tomatoes (the only kind the cook could raise in Alaska), he packed the tomatoes into sterilized quart jars with a pinch of dill, added one tablespoon of salt, a lump of alum the size of a bantam egg and a quarter cup of vinegar and filled the jar with boiling water before sealing it.

Although I did not taste these green miniatures, they looked tempting on the shelves. That remarkable man had thirty-eight varieties of his pickled ingenuity on display, and each jar was a work of art. He told me he made his own vinegar by allowing white raisin jack to go sour, then straining, settling and bottling the pale liquid.

I make a topaz vinegar by mashing one-half peck of persimmons in a crock and adding two gallons of warm water, one-and-one-half pounds of sugar and a package of yeast that has been dissolved with a teaspoon of sugar in a cup of warm water. I let the liquid ferment and when the mushy pulp stops its labored bubbling, I strain, settle and siphon it into bottles. I cork it lightly and when a mother forms, I cork it tightly for storage.

To create an herb vinegar that teases fresh-leaf salads, combine one cup of vinegar with two tablespoons of onion juice, a teaspoon of chopped mint leaves, a quarter of a teaspoon each of crushed, dried chervil, marjoram and tarragon. Shake every day for four days, strain, store and use as needed.

I drizzle herb vinegar on mustard salad that my gentle Georgia neighbor told me about: chop one cup of young mustard leaves, add one-half teaspoon of minced onion, a teaspoon of olive oil, a tablespoon of sugar and a pinch of salt. Zesty, different and stimulating!

Vinegar has not been restricted to flavoring and preserving. In many homes vinegar was considered to be a purifier. My grandparents were not regarded as unusual for their belief that the odor of rotting cabbages and apples caused "spring diseases," nor was their use of vinegar water to scrub the offending bins thought to be out of the ordinary. I use vinegar water to clean the dog run—not to combat disease but to make the area smell better. My neighbor cleans her refrigerator with vinegar water and my daughter sometimes rinses her hair in diluted vinegar.

Herbal doctors and Indians have recommended the use of

vinegar mixtures in medicine. I knew a real-live Indian medicine man who "pickled the medicines of the earth, put ferment into a body, and drove out evil" with vinegar concoctions.

The Indian, named Peter, prescribed exercise "motion for stability," all kinds of baths (alkaline, acid, sitz, head, foot), good food, tonics (gentian root, ash bark or black pepper in wine), but for specific problems he "shook his herbs in vinegar," and he called them pickled. Listed below are some of Indian Peter's recommendations:

Anisestar, "shook" in white vinegar, rids the bones of tiredness if a teaspoonful is taken three times a day.

Anise vinegar, sniffed vigorously, will control sneezing.

Caraway in vinegar, rubbed on the skin, will dispel wax and allow the flesh to sweat.

Cinnamon sticks infused in half vinegar and half hot water, taken internally, will dry the blood and make a man thin.

Cloves that have been pickled in vinegar must be sucked to sweeten a young girl's breath and make her attractive to boys.

Coriander seeds "shook" in vinegar will prevent heartburn if taken after a rich meal (one teaspoon of the liquid is sipped slowly).

Curry in vinegar, a teaspoonful four times a day, will cool a fever.

Dill herb pickled in vinegar, nibbled, will slow heart palpitations after running.

Fennel vinegar taken internally sharpens the eyesight. "Snakes eat fennel to sharpen their vision."

Garlic when infused in vinegar and taken internally dulls the senses but strengthens the body.

Ginger root shaken in vinegar (a teaspoonful taken three times a day) quiets the heart.

Horseradish in vinegar, when used as a hot soak, helps to soften corns on the feet and relieve tiredness.

Mace pickled in wine vinegar (two ounces sipped at bedtime) cures sleeplessness.

Mustard seeds "shook" in vinegar will pep you up and make you breathe deeply.

Onions in vinegar (eat the onions) are very good for the eyes; onions rest the eyes when they are tired.

Pepper in diluted vinegar, a tablespoonful each day for a month, will "make a man a man."

Pickle Power

Poppy seeds pickled in vinegar make a man sleep.

Rosemary and sage in vinegar make an excellent hair rinse.

Salt soothes. Peter made various kinds of salty vinegars. Salt in vinegar will relieve an ache in muscles. Taken internally, salty vinegar will "regulate."

Saltpeter in vinegar slows emotions, "very small spoon" as needed.

Thyme preserved in vinegar, taken internally, expels phlegm.

Wild rocket pickled in vinegar makes breathing easier and gives new life to old people when taken in the early spring.

Indian Peter had many more spices and herbs that he "shook," but the most inspiring part of his "medicine" was his personal concern for every person who came to him for advice. He firmly believed that he was responsible to all men; he believed that everyone "should have time for, and wait on one another." He did not believe in the Devil, saying that the civilized world had created the Devil and that the real demon in man was heartlessness, "unfeeling toward others."

Knowing Peter's wife, seeing her great smile, feeling her pride in her husband's art, was an uplifting experience in itself. One day she called me to her house and declared in her generous-spirited way that she was going to teach me to make catsup. She knew that my husband had a real passion for catsup and that I dutifully tried to please him. She also knew that the last three years I made catsup I burned it. For me, catsup defies the big rule of cooking, "Relax." It is impossible to relax with catsup. It is an attention-hungry, insubordinate, insecure relish that is easily alienated. It sulks on the bottom of the pan and burns for me, I told her, but while I protested, while I kept shaking my head, she handed me the big knife and told me to chop eighteen ripe tomatoes, six large onions and three big peppers, which she swept off my board and cooked for twenty minutes. While it was boiling, she added two-and-a-half cups of vinegar, three teaspoons of salt, one cup of sugar, two teaspoons of cinnamon, one teaspoon of allspice and a little cloves and nutmeg. It boiled slowly for three-quarters of an hour more while we drank coffee. Then she poured the thick, lumpy catsup into hot, sterilized jars and sealed them at once.

I took some home and served it for supper with Polish Sausage, which Lewis loves sopped in catsup. He pronounced our product warm-hearted and outgoing, with the spicy, friendly overtones of our good neighbor.

Vinegar is often used as an acid additive to enhance the preserving qualities of fruits and vegetables. Vinegar pickles are fickle phonies but flavorful fun; even I can create palatable vinegar pickles.

For Counterfeit Cuques, select cucumbers about two inches long, wash, and soak overnight in a salt brine made of one-half pound salt dissolved in two quarts of water. Remove the cucumbers the following day and plunge them into clear, cold water. Dry the Cuques and fit them to fill sterilized pint jars. Heat one quart of vinegar, one-quarter ounce of stick cinnamon, one ounce of mustard seed and four pounds of brown sugar to the boiling point, pour over the cucumbers and seal at once. Keep nimble fingers out of these sweet pickles for at least two weeks.

Pickled blackberries make a tasty relish. Dissolve four pounds of sugar in one-and-one-half cups of vinegar, add one teaspoon each of cinnamon and cloves, and a pinch of salt and pepper. Boil and when the sugar has dissolved add six pounds of large, firm blackberries. Cook slowly for forty minutes. Do not stir. Pour into hot, sterilized jars and seal.

Peaches, pears, grapes, cherries, crabapples and plums may be pickled in much the same manner but be sure to prick the skins of whole fruits or they will explode, turn into mush, and you will end up with seedy pickled jam.

Anne's Pickled Chutney may be made with apples or pears, and its strumpet spirit kids mutton into thinking it's lamb. Wash, pare, quarter and core five pounds of firm, ripe pears or apples (or mix them). Stir in one-half cup of minced green pepper, one-and-one-half cups of raisins, four cups of sugar, one cup of crystallized ginger that has been cut very thin, one orange ground with its peeling, three cups of vinegar, one-half teaspoon of salt and one cup of water. Bring to a boil while you tie one-quarter teaspoon each of powdered cloves, nutmeg and allspice, six bay leaves and a teaspoon of cinnamon in a piece of cloth. Immerse the spice bag into the fruit, lower the fire, and simmer until the chutney is thick and brown. Marvelous odors will envelop your block when you stir the chutney, but do not bend to temptation and give it all away to the crowds that follow their noses and flock to your door. Spoon into sterilized pint jars, seal and save your chutney for your sweetie.

Pickle Power

In Alaska we used to pickle mushrooms in half-pint jars, and when we had roast moose we would garnish the meat with these piquant buttons of tart happiness. Boil one cup of vinegar with one-half cup of water and two teaspoons of salt, together with two whole cloves, two whole black peppercorns, two crushed cloves of garlic and a bay leaf all tied in a cloth. Pop in about a pound of washed, big fresh mushrooms. Simmer for five minutes and when the mushrooms have shrunk to proper tidbit size, fish them out with a slotted spoon and transfer them to hot, sterilized jars. Bring the vinegar to a boil again and fill each jar of mushrooms with the boiling liquid. Spoon one teaspoon of olive oil onto the top of each jar and seal. Try to keep pickled mushrooms for two weeks before eating them.

Whether you are a fermenter of the old salt school, a salt-and-vinegar advocate or a fickle pickler, the variety of potential pickles on this earth is endless. Even the least lovely produce may be transformed into table treats by pickling and the lowliest is exalted when it becomes a means of saving God's gifts from the land.

8

Just Naturally Potted

I cannot think of potted foods without remembering our cow, Lucky Strike, and her contribution to the grand potted cheeses of our home. Lucky Strike had always been a good milker but had never been an overly motherly mother—in fact, she seemed glad to be rid of her offspring. She would prefer hanging her head over the fence and begging for a fag. Lucky Strike learned to enjoy tobacco in her youth before Granddaddy bought her from a family of shiftless farmfolk. Hooked on the habit, Lucky would try to go right through the fence to get either chewing tobacco or cigarettes. Sometimes neighbor boys would slip her a pinch of roll-your-own, then substitute a lighted cigarette. She didn't seem to mind a little smoke curling around her nostrils. But we did. Whenever Lucky Strike ate tobacco, her milk tasted like old cigars for a week.

One year Grandma decided to make this tobacco-flavored milk into cheese; that was a blooper. Then Grandma potted some of the nicotine spread. That was worse. Generally speaking, however, Grandma's potted cheeses were superb.

Potted means preserved in pots, usually with salt or fat. Men first potted meat by cooking it, packing it into earthen pots, then covering it with fat to make the container airtight. Vegetables such as beans, corn, green tomatoes, beets, and greens such as chard and spinach, have been potted by mixing them with one-fourth their weight of salt (or brine strong enough to prevent all bacterial action), then protecting the surface of the pot with a covering of paraffin. Fish and fowl have been preserved by pressing the cooked and boned pulp into stoneware pots and sealing the potted meat with fat. Cheese has been preserved in sealed pots since Biblical times.

Most cheeses are formed by bacteria in milk that turn milk sugars into lactic acids which unite with casein to curdle milk. Bacteria, like other microorganisms, require heat, moisture and food to survive. Bacteria are the activists in the fermentation process that changes milk to cheese. In addition to natural souring agents, cheese makers often introduce special bacteria into clabber to flavor the cheese. The fungi feed on lactic acids of the curd and give the cheese a specific taste and texture.

Checking bacterial growth in cheese after it has cured is just as important as inducing fermentation, and potting is one way to stop most bacterial action and to preserve cheese.

The steps in cheese making are: coagulating or curdling the milk, stirring and heating the curd, draining off the whey, collecting or pressing the curd, salting, curing the cheese (holding the cheese for a specified time at a certain temperature and humidity), and sealing it.

Extreme cleanliness should be observed at all stages of cheese making, Grandma advised, saying that vagrant molds were always lurking around milk products looking for a handout.

One of the "glories of curd," as my grandmother would say, is that no two cheese-making methods and no two cheeses are exactly the same. Although the details of setting the milk and other steps are varied, all natural cheeses are created by a similar process: that of fermentation. As in brewing and meat curing, with fermentation there is a pledge of faith in the future; there is a tomorrow when a cycle of life is enacted.

Though oversimplified, a cheese classification might read:

I. Soft, unripened, such as clabber, cottage or cream cheese.
   Soft, ripened with mold, such as Camembert.
II. Semisoft, ripened with blue mold, such as Roquefort.
   Semisoft, ripened by bacteria and surface microorganisms, such as Limburger or Port Salut.
   Semisoft, ripened by bacteria, such as brick or Munster.
III. Hard, with eyes, ripened by bacteria, such as Swiss or Gruyère.

Hard, without eyes, ripened by bacteria, such as Cheddar.
IV. Very hard, ripened by bacteria, such as Parmesan.

Utensils required for making and potting foods need not be
elaborate. The main essential is a pot to put it in. Years ago
crockery pots of all sizes and shapes were used. I find that old
lidded sugar bowls are fine for tiny batches of potted foods and
that plastic cottage cheese cartons are excellent for larger pots.
Metal is not recommended for either containers or tools. A colander, large enamel kettles, wooden spoons and boards, and a food
thermometer are useful. Cheesecloth or muslin, paraffin or lard
are also used in the potting of specific foods.

For making cheese, the basic ingredient is milk (whole, skim,
evaporated milk or cream). Rennet is often used as a coagulant
of the casein in milk. Animal rennet is made from a substance
in the stomach of calves and lambs and it is marketed as a
liquid, solid or powder. Vegetable rennets are made from plants
such as the thistle, nettle or bedstraw. Commercial rennet may
be purchased at most grocery stores.

Making cheese in dibs and dabs is really a fun chore. I have
my little cheese-making cloths, actually squares of muslin, and
nearly every week there is a ball of curd hanging from the
faucet on the kitchen sink. I covet spore and inoculate geriatric
milk or reconstituted dry skim milk whenever I discover a new
fermentum. Most often I start my clabber by sneaking a couple
of spoonfuls of commercial sour cream, buttermilk, cottage
cheese, or yogurt happiness into a quart of milk. Then I let my
imagination take over. Sometimes, after a day or two, or perhaps four or five, I dump my clabber into a kettle of water (hot
to the touch, 110° F.), set for twenty-five minutes and drain the
whey. Sometimes I submerge a sack of clabber in hot water,
100° to 110° F., for a few minutes, then hang it to drain on the
kitchen faucet. I have even heated the clabber directly over a
fire, but that's tricky and scorched curd is a "defilement of ferment!" my grandmother raved one time when she smelled my
mistake. If you do not wish to defile your ferment, pour the
clabber into water and heat it to 110° F.

The great thing about housewifely play with ferment is the
sport of the game; like other offspring, no two products are
identical and more often than not they surprise you by their
goodness.

Schmierkase, a simple, uncured cheese Grandma made out of whole milk (I use skim milk), may be eaten immediately or cured into Farmer cheese by sealing it in pots. Grandma made Schmierkase and Farmer cheese out of morning milk which she said was richer because Lucky Strike did nothing but chew all night and "think rich." Granddaddy agreed, saying that although idleness was usually the parent of want, idle cud chewing was necessary for a cow.

After the milk had been strained, but before it had set, Grandma poured about a gallon of it into an enamel pan, and added a little buttermilk or a teaspoon of dried rennet. She let the milk stand in a warm room (75° to 85° F.) for six hours, then cut the curd into one-inch pieces before putting the enamel pan into hot water. The water was heated to "fever" (100° to 104° F.) and held until the curd temperature reached about 90° F. She put a double thickness of cheesecloth in the colander and drained the whey off the curd. She tied the corners of the cheesecloth and hung the cheese on the faucet to drip for about five minutes. The ball of cheese, still encased in cloth, was then rinsed by dipping it up and down in cold water. The cheese was hung to drip a second time, and when it stopped draining, Grandma emptied it onto a board and worked it with a fork to remove all the whey.

For Schmierkase the curd was simply worked with a fork, salted, and if it seemed dry, a little cream or butter was added before the cheese was covered and refrigerated. A heaping bowl of Schmierkase was regularly served for lunch, plain or seasoned with parsley, chervil, chives, tarragon, sorrel or cress. I loved Schmierkase and cress sandwiches. Sometimes Grandma spooned fruit (preserved, fresh or stewed in red wine) over unsalted Schmierkase for a lovely, soft dessert.

For Farmer cheese (or potted Schmierkase) Grandma took more care to work all the droplets of whey from the curd because she said that they would ferment and cause acidity. Sometimes she placed the bag of curd between two boards and pressed out the whey or she left the cheese under the pressure of the boards overnight. The next morning she salted the cheese and pressed it into a sterilized earthenware pot, salted the top, lidded the container and sealed the lid with paraffin. Potted Farmer cheese was held in Granddaddy's wine cellar, a misty-moisty, dark and spidery dungeon in a room off the base of the stairs where the temperatures remained about 50° to 60° F. Farmer cheese was usually made in the spring when Lucky Strike was fresh and it was eaten the following winter. Pale, dry and flat, Farmer cheese was sliced for nibbles while we talked around the table after supper. It was an even-tempered cheese and seemed content to be a placid tidbit.

Cheese dumplings may be made with Schmierkase or the potted Farmer cheese. Mash one pound of cheese, add four slightly beaten eggs, eight heaping tablespoons of flour and one-half teaspoon of salt. Mash together until smooth. Wet your hands and form the dough into balls. Drop the two-inch round dumplings into two quarts of salted boiling water, cover and cook for twenty minutes. Drain the cooked dumplings, then put them into slightly browned breadcrumbs (about one-half cup of breadcrumbs toasted in two or three tablespoons of butter) in the skillet. Roll and turn the dumplings until they are spangled with the golden-brown crumbs and serve at once.

One autumn night when the world was carpeted in bronze and gold and a great moon shafted its light as if trying to illuminate that tapestry of color, I remember hurrying home, pushing open the kitchen door and encountering the steamy fragrance of sauerkraut, spareribs, cheese dumplings and pineapple pie. The joy of that moment was, as someone said, "the highest synthesis of life: consciousness, compassion and gratefulness to God." A heaping platter of cheese dumplings is the synthesis of hearty early American food.

I have made Farmer cheese (and Schmierkase) from homogenized commercial milk. Sometimes it turned out good, but once in a while I end up with pebble-sized rubber balls. My problem may have been temperature, disadvantaged fungi, the wrong sign of the moon, or milker's wart; warts are said to sour milk the "wrong way." My neighbor said that my leather-tough cheese was caused because the milk did not contain enough fat.

If fresh or opened potted cheese became acid, my grandmother reworked it with cream, then wrapped it in cheesecloth that had been dipped in wine and layered hops around the ball. The cheese was wrapped in paper and refrigerated until we ate it. Actually the aromatic reworked cheeses were as delicious as the first time around.

My grandmother often repeated that "cheeses do not spoil,"

which I took to mean that cheese would not poison, so I have clabbered and curded with a light heart.

For a rich, moist, plain potted cheese, Grandma allowed sour cream to thicken in a warm place for three or four days. She set the colander in the large mixing bowl in the sink, and draped a cheesecloth over it, then she poured the clabbered cream into the cloth and immediately emptied a teakettleful of boiling water over the sour cream. Grandma cut the spout of boiling water back and forth across the clabber, let the cheese set in the hot water for five minutes, then pulled up the corners of the cheesecloth to let the cheese drain by overnight hanging.

The following morning she turned the yellow cheese into a bowl and mashed it smooth with a fork as she added enough thick sweet or sour cream to bring it to a soft butter-like consistency. She seasoned the cheese with salt to taste and packed it tightly with a spoon into a clean cheesecloth square which was draped over a bowl. The bowl was a little smaller than the crock in which she planned to pot the cheese. She tied and trimmed the cheesecloth sack, layered salt in the bottom of the potting crock, then put the sacked cheese into the sterilized crock, and packed salt around it and across the top. Grandma sealed the crock with a layer of paraffin, paraffined the jar lid tight, and stored the cheese in a cool place at approximately 50° F.

When we broke out a cheese one to three months later, it was firm but mellow, riddled with small holes and blessed with character. Grandma called this soft cheese simply "potted," but I have tasted a commercial salt cheese named Feta that was very similar in flavor.

Kochkase was a regular patron of our potting crocks when Lucky Strike was not on strike; actually a cooked cheese, Kochkase was ripened and often flavored before it was sealed in pots. Grandma clabbered whole milk in an enamel pan by adding a teaspoon of rennet and allowing the milk to stand in a warm place for six hours. She placed the pan in hot water (100° to 104° F.) for five or ten minutes and while the clabber was warming she cut the curd. Grandma drained the cheese through a double cheesecloth in the colander in the sink, tied the cloth and dripped the cheese curd before rinsing it in cold water. She then emptied the cheese onto a board and worked out the whey by mashing the cheese with a fork. Kochkase must be chopped very fine, she said, before returning it to a crock to cure, covered in a warm place, for three or four days. The length of time required to "ripen" depends upon the temperature and the moisture content of the curd. If the cheese is held at 70° F., ripening will take a week; at 80° F., Kochkase curd will cure in about five days. For a milder product the cheese should be held for a shorter time in cure at higher temperature, my grandmother advised. The cheese begins to ripen when the top layer wrinkles or becomes moldy.

Although some people do not flavor Kochkase my grandmother added a pinch of cumin to the curd, then poured the entire mass into the enamel pan and heated it over a slow fire to 180° F. Grandma stirred it constantly for about thirty minutes, and when the cheese became as slickety smooth as egg white she poured it back into the washed and sterilized crock and covered it. After the cheese cooled it was eaten or lidded, sealed with paraffin and stored for a month at 50° to 60° F.

Plain, Kochkase tasted somewhat like Camembert; flavored with cumin, it reminded me of dirty feet and I couldn't get past the smell, but my grandfather certainly enjoyed his Kochkase and beer.

Controlling each step of cheese making results in a uniform product, but part of the fun in potting homemade cheese is variety. With cheese, I often feel like the lady of the street who remarked, "I don't know where I'm going till I get there, but afterwards I sure know where I've been." Potting cheese adds a touch of mystery to the natural life.

When my grandmother felt expansive she mashed small pieces of naturally fermented commercial cheese with her homemade cheese, then "ripened" or cured the combination for a few days at room temperature, and sealed her product in pots. When opened, her plagiarized cheese had not only assumed part of the borrowed flavor, but had developed a unique personality all its own.

Grandma named some of her cheeses after the store from which she purchased her commercial contributions, and she called one Gyp Joint. We kept old Gyp Joint's spore around for a long time because she kept inoculating new cheeses with the old.

Blue, or Fromage Bleu, as we called Roquefort-type cheeses, was inoculated with *Penicillium roquefortii* mold, and Grandma, a cheese plagiarist of the most innocent kind, crumbled a bit of commercial blue into her homemade product.

For her own Fromage Bleu she clabbered whole milk with rennet, cut and heated the curd to 90° F., and after her new cheese had drained overnight by hanging in the sack, she salted it to taste, added a teaspoon of crumbled blue cheese and a quarter-cup of butter to each cup of cheese, then mashed and mixed it well. She transferred the cheese back to its sack and hung it in a cool cellar for ten days, rubbing salt on the outside of the cheesecloth sack each day. Grandma then pricked the balled cheese all over with her knitting needle because she told me that air must reach the inside of the cheese for blue mold to grow. The Fromage Bleu was cured for about three months by hanging in the cellar, and if mold or slime formed on the sack, she scraped it off. Bleu cheese may be eaten any time after it is cured, but Grandma usually potted several balls by packing them in crocks of salt and sealing the tops with paraffin. If held in an airtight container at temperatures of about 45° to 55° F., Fromage Bleu does not deteriorate, she said.

Grandma made a potted Belle Curd, as she called it, which was slightly gray but beautifully mild and sweet to taste. In a double boiler, at a temperature of 104° to 110° F., she curdled a pan of "evening milk" (which she said was less rich than Lucky Strike's morning milk) by adding a cup or so of soured clabber. Lowering the fire under the double boiler, she cut the curd into one-half inch squares and stirred it carefully. When the curd was firm but not rubbery, she drained off the whey through cheesecloth, then put the cloth-covered curd on a board, placed a second board on top, pressed it to squeeze out the whey. She tied the corners of the cheesecloth and let the cheese hang in a warm place (80° F.) overnight. The next morning Grandma salted her cheese fairly heavily and kneaded the curd with her hands. Returning the cheese to its cloth sack she hung it for twelve hours in a brine that floated an egg (one pound of salt dissolved in about a gallon of water). The cheese was then dried and cured in the refrigerator for three weeks. She turned the cheeses once a week and salted them lightly, and when the curing time was up she cleaned off excess slime or mold and potted them individually in crocks of salt. They were sealed with paraffin and allowed to ripen for at least three months in a cool, dark place. Grandma served Belle Curd in sandwiches and casseroles.

All sorts of wild flavors may be added to the basic potted cheese, and the results are always a surprise. For a cheddar flavor Grandma kneaded in a wee bit of Madeira-type wine. Mace, an infinitesimal amount, gives a subtle taste of well-aged cheese. Mustard gives a tangy, sharp flavor. A handful of caraway seeds somehow hints of Holland and windmills. Cayenne pepper worked in with a little butter adds color and a spirited flavor. It is practically impossible to spoil potted cheese, my grandmother said.

Grandma added chopped ingredients to some of her cheeses before potting them, and the texture change was pleasant; hickory nuts and ground black walnuts were cheery in cheese; crumbled dried clover leaves added a hayfield flavor; and dried summer sausage in potted cheese was wonderful.

Grandma made a counterfeit Limburger cheese that rivaled the smelliest on the market. When her pots of Limburger were almost used up, she would go down to the Gyp Joint and pinch and smell all the strong cheeses on the shelf. Armed with all the intestinal fortitude her tiny self could gather, she would march up to the counter carrying several foil-wrapped cheeses and ask the butcher to open those with the stoutest odors. She would select the cheese with the deepest red-yellow pigment and slimiest surface. It always embarrassed me to ride the streetcar with Grandma when she had shopped at the Gyp Joint. Passengers moved away from us.

At home Grandma heated whole milk to about 90° F. and added a tablespoon of rennet, stirred the milk and turned off the fire. About thirty minutes later she cut the curd into one-half-inch squares to insure that it was sufficiently firm, then drained off the whey through cheesecloth stretched over the colander. Gathering up the four corners of the cloth she dipped the curd up and down in a weak, cold-water brine (three-eighths cup of salt dissolved in one-half gallon of water). She pressed the ball of cheese between two boards to express the whey, emptied it onto the breadboard and shaped the curd into three-inch cubes. She sprinkled dry salt on each surface, packed the squares closely together in dry salt on the big board for one day at room temperature, then brushed the salt from them and rubbed every surface of each cheese with the slimy yellow surface bacteria and yeasts from the ripe commercial Limburger that she had purchased.

The whole block knew when Grandma was making Limburger. The high odor drew dogs and cats from miles around, and they would perch in trees and fight on the ground; this animal convention went on for three days while my unimpressed grandmother ripened her cheeses on the shelf behind the stove. She rubbed the cheeses with the "boughten" Limburger rind, and turned them two or three times a day for three days.

The cheese was next rubbed with salt, put in mason jars, tightly lidded and laid in the refrigerator to cure for two or three weeks. Grandma then removed the cheese, wrapped each piece in wax paper and tinfoil, and potted the foil cubes of cheese. To do this, she packed the cubes in the crocks, lidded them and sealed each container with paraffin. She cured her homemade Limburger for at least sixty days in the cool, dark basement and when she broke one out, it was terrific. The surface inoculated microorganisms ripened the semisoft cheese and the mellow, salty-acid flavor permeated every pore and opening. Our house was very popular when Granddaddy cracked a pot of Limburger; the visitors would bring their kids and we'd play in the back yard while the grownups sat on the veranda swing or in rockers and enjoyed the sweet evening air. The air smells so good after a mouthful of Limburger.

My family has never had enough spare milk to indulge in extensive cheese potting, but if we ever get a cow (which Lewis says will be never), I'll try lots of Grandma's potted pleasures. Even in suburbia, however, I do sneak a few of her ideas into our icebox. I empty a can of evaporated milk into a pint jar or carton, add two or three teaspoons of commercial sour cream, fill the container with whole milk, stir it, cover and let it set at room temperature for two or three days. When it's well clabbered, I heat it to 110° F. by pouring it into a skillet of warm water. I drape cheesecloth over the colander in the sink and empty the heated clabber into it. Next I salt the cheese, draw up the corners of the cloth and submerge the sack in warm water (100° F.) for five or ten minutes. I then let the cheese drip. When it is well drained, I pour it into a bowl, mash it with a fork, and add a teaspoon or two of crumbled blue cheese, Camembert, Munster or any other naturally ripened cheese whose flavor I wish to liberate. I put my inoculated cheese into a couple of old sugar bowls with lids and leave them at room temperature for two or three days. Mold sometimes grows, sometimes slime wrinkles across the top. I mix it into the cheese, taste for saltiness (it should be a bit more salty than you wish the finished product to be), then I lid each container and tie each bowl in a plastic bread wrapper. My cheeses are stored in the bottom of the icebox for two or three weeks to ripen, and though not as full-bodied as my grandmother's, most of them are very good.

On the spur of the moment last summer our family decided to rise at four A.M. and climb Old Rag, a stony mountain near our place at Boston, Virginia. Breakfast on the mountaintop! It sounded like a great idea the night before. We were the only car on the road and the only group on the trail as we started up in the mist that moved dismally through the trees. I was dismal myself because the only thing I could find for our mountaintop breakfast was a loaf of bread, peanuts and a bowl of cheese. I didn't dare tell the family of our poor fare in the light of our less-than-spirited surroundings. When we reached the top the weather was worse. Wind scudded grayness around the boulders, and we could see neither up, out nor down. There was a frosty silence as we huddled to open the packsack, and when I pulled out our breakfast, Lewis questioned "Is that all?" I had the feeling that if the children had known which way to push me, they would have. We couldn't see anything. Then, just as I opened the bread, as suddenly as a bolt of lightning, the clouds opened up. We were bathed in sunlight, sitting amid lichen-covered boulders with glistening plants and sparkling little pools on every side. Suddenly it was seven o'clock in the morning. We tore into the bread, smeared it with cheese, and loved it. We bounced like puppies back down the mountain, spreading peanut shells, drinking water from the springs and drinking in the beautiful, beautiful world about us. It was eight-and-a-half miles back to the car around the base of the mountain. We washed in a stream and drove up to a lodge for lunch at one-thirty. As it happened, the D. A. R. was engaged in a meeting there, and when we filed in we heard the speaker emote, "Storms roar against the shoulders of our country but the lightning only serves to show the glories of our nation."

We five—bedraggled, a little beragged—loaded our plates at

the buffet and sat in another area. We could hear the colorful words and we knew what those ladies were talking about. We had been to the top of the mountain and we had seen the glories of our land unfold beneath us. We had tasted the earth's goodness through our eyes, our ears and our flesh, and through a little pot of cheese.

Cheese is not the only farm food that may be potted, and not all potted produce is content to make a pleasant pot. I potted cheap eggs once but neglected the paraffin. Green, hairy salt and lightweight eggs persuaded me to throw out the mess. Months earlier I had bragged to Lewis about how good it felt to have seven or eight dozen eggs in the basement, but I am glad I did not have to depend on those hairy little creatures. Sealing potted produce is an important part of potting.

Across a hump of land from Bear Glacier near Seward, Alaska, where, in 1794, the Russians built their first North American sailing vessel, a clear trout stream dashes to the Pacific. I once knew a laughing, red-headed Englishman who placer-mined rice gold on that creek. Every summer he would seine the green and orange polka-dotted Arctic char that schooled awaiting the late salmon run. I had a weekend panning operation on a nearby creek and my neighbor used to visit me when I walked up the coast to pan an ounce or two. He told me about an English breakfast dish he called potted char.

To pot the char, he cleaned and boiled the fish right on the seashore, and when they were mushy soft he cooled them, removed the skin and bones with his fingers, pressed the fish with a sprinkling of salt into a crockery casserole, and when the container was packed about three-fourths full of pulpy fish, he melted butter and poured it over them. He set the crock in a large pan of water, heated to boiling, lidded the pan and simmered it overnight. The following day he poured a layer of paraffin over the fish, lidded the pot with metal, and carried it to a nearby cave for storage. His cave, a cleft in the rocks, must have reached through the mountain to Bear Glacier, because a steady, icy flow of air breathed from the black crevasse.

My English miner acquaintance said that he ate potted char fried with mashed potatoes, and that a breakfast of char put him in good humor all day long. I can still hear his laugh, and though I did not taste the fish, I remember his ebullience and high spirit.

Modern, hermetically sealed meat-canning methods were invented two hundred years ago; before that time meats to be kept were salted, dried or potted. Although potting cooked meats (usually the smaller and less-than-elegant pieces) was a common housewifely chore, Grandmother did not pot meat, but she did pot chicken.

My grandmother had no patience with people or hens who did not do their job. If one of her hens fell down on the egg-making job, Grandma potted her.

After carefully determining who was, and who was not, laying, Grandma snatched the wayward hen from her roost at night and put the sleepy creature in a crate. The following morning she heated a teakettle of water to boiling and, armed with a hatchet, marched to the "killing spot" between the garages. There, she poured the hot water into a five-gallon can, grabbed the hen, slipped its head between two upright nails in the chopping block, stretched its neck and whop! With one motion she half-hitched a short rope around one of the chicken's legs and hung the bird upside down against the garage, holding the neck for a minute so that there would be no splatter. Next, she submerged the chicken in the hot water for one minute, then re-hung the wet bird by one foot and plucked its feathers, starting at its legs and plucking downward toward the neck. Clean breast feathers were tucked into a burlap sack hanging nearby (for pillow stuffing) and the tough old feathers went into a bag for disposal. From time to time she rinsed her hands in water because feathers stick like crazy. After pulling out any pinfeathers with a blunt knife, Grandma washed the feet and brought the plucked hen to the kitchen to singe off the hairs over the cookstove fire.

Next she "drew" the bird, first slitting the skin from breastbone to vent and cutting out around the vent. Then inserting her hand into the cavity along the inside of the rib cage, she pulled out the innards. Carefully, Grandma removed the gizzard, heart and liver and cut the greenish gall sack away from the liver. She removed lungs and then she reached way in, to the base of the bird's neck, for the craw. Taking a turn around the "windpipe" with her index finger, she gingerly withdrew the craw and pipes.

The hen was then washed and ready to pot.

For potting chicken, Grandma put the cut-up bird and giblets into an old-fashioned stone jar and covered it with water. She added one bay leaf and salt and pepper to taste, then lidded the jar and simmered it overnight (or until the meat fell from the bones) in a slow oven. She drained the chicken (saving the liquid), boned it, discarded excessive skin and fat, removed the giblets, and cubed the chicken meat.

In a skillet she fried two chopped onions until they were transparent, added one-and-one-half cups of canned tomatoes, a sprig of chopped parsley and a small can of drained and minced pimientos. She simmered these vegetables together with the chicken stock for about thirty minutes, or until it had been reduced by about a third, emptied the cubed chicken meat into the mushy liquid, brought it to a boil and poured the whole thing back into the stone jar.

The potted chicken was lidded and cooked in a slow oven for six or eight hours, then cooled and refrigerated. For longer keeping, the layer of chicken fat on top of the crock was covered with melted paraffin and the lid sealed with paraffin.

The potted chicken was kept in a cool place and once opened, it was refrigerated. To serve, we broke the seal, scraped off the heavy layer of fat, and cut out chunks of the colorful jelly and pretty cubed meat. With toast or hot biscuits, a green salad and cottage cheese pie, potted hen was superb.

My grandmother had two brothers. Fritz raised peaches in southern Missouri; he was an old-maid bachelor, exacting and difficult, but after he died and left a chunk of cash to his numerous nephews and nieces, his name was spoken with reverence. Otto raised pigs and fourteen youngsters in northwest Missouri, and I remember him with warm feelings. They say the spirit is ennobled by the memory of a good man.

Uncle Otto seemed to have been deprived of all the joys of life. As a child he was sickly, stooped in stature, and ignored by everyone except his mother. Though secure in the old country as a bookkeeper, when his mother died he followed Grandma, Fritz and Aunt Rosie to America, where he secured work as a clerk in a mill and lived alone in a big old house north of St. Joseph. Few people were more than superficially agreeable toward him, because they could not see beyond his deformity. Nevertheless, Uncle Otto extended kindness to others and was always ready to help if he could. He held a deep trust in God and often dropped into the church during his solitary excursions.

One day at the church a funeral was in progress and as he knelt he saw a widow slumped in resignation beside a string of fourteen pale, silently wretched children. In the days that followed he learned that the family was almost destitute; the father and husband had been a railroad man whose legs had been severed in an accident after which he had lingered for months, taxing every resource of his farm before he died.

Uncle Otto undertook to pay the family's debts and to restore their credit with tradesmen; and when the widow discovered the name of her benefactor, she came with two of her children to thank him. Her children, frightened at first of the hunchback, soon responded to Otto's gentle, bright mind, and before long his house came alive with young people running in and out. They came to look on him with affection and no longer saw his deformity.

Otto and the widow, Aunt Clair, were married, and though some people clucked tongues at the match, Otto loved and "raised his children." All fourteen learned a trade or went to at least two years of college. Later in life, when asked how he managed, Uncle Otto looked up fondly at his wife and muttered, "Clair und speck."

Aunt Clair was a whiz with a pot and possessed a talent for creating tasty dishes out of scraps of meat. They had quite a few hogs butchered every fall, and she cured the larger pieces, then potted the trimmings.

For plain potted pork, she simmered about ten pounds of trim from jowl, Boston butt, neckbones and shanks along with two tablespoons of salt, two bay leaves, a whole lemon thinly sliced, a quart of beer and water to cover. When the bones came free and the meat was very tender, she boned it and discarded the gristle, tissue, fat and skin. While boning the meat she reduced three cups of the stock to about one-half. She pulled the meat apart with a fork and seasoned it with one teaspoon of whole black peppercorns, a crushed clove of garlic, and two teaspoons of salt. She mixed one-and-one-half cups of reduced stock with one-half cup of beer and stirred it into the meat. She then poured the sloppy meat into a dry potting crock that had been sterilized by boiling. After slowly heating the potted meat in the oven to 225° F., she kept it, uncovered, at that temperature for four hours. She lidded and cooled the pot in the oven, heat off, overnight. The next morning Aunt Clair sealed the meat with at least two inches of melted lard or one inch of paraffin. She chilled the crock overnight in the ice house and the next day sealed the top a second time with melted paraffin. She lidded the crock securely and stored it in a cool place. Potted pork may be scooped out of the pot, sliced, and served cold as a luncheon meat. It may be sliced, floured and slowly fried until brown and crusty. Once opened, potted meat must be stored in the icebox.

My grandmother used to serve Aunt Clair's fried potted pork with a tart horseradish sauce, which she made by cooking together in a heavy saucepan one tablespoon each of butter and flour, to which she added a cup of boiling water and two teaspoons of vinegar. Grandma stirred the sauce until it was thick and smooth, and just before she took it from the fire she folded in a tablespoon of grated horseradish and a cup of sour cream. Poured over the crisp-fried potted pork, her sour gravy added zip to the meat.

Aunt Clair potted pork tongue by rubbing ten pounds of fresh tongues with a dry cure made of one scant teaspoon of saltpeter, one cup of salt, and eight tablespoons of sugar. She laid the tongues in a crock to weep for two weeks, then rinsed them, soaked them for thirty minutes in fresh water, changed the water, and boiled them until very tender. She cleaned, peeled, and finely chopped the tongues together with one pound of fresh lard. With a fork she mashed and mixed in a little black pepper, nutmeg, mace and a sprinkle of crushed red pepper pods. She packed the meat into sterilized crockery pots, carefully pushing it down into every corner, covered the tops with a little melted lard and baked them in a slow oven (225° degrees F.) for two hours. The pots were refrigerated overnight to shrink, then sealed with two inches of melted lard and tightly lidded. The tin lids "keep the varmints out and the good pigs' tongue in," she used to say, winking as she asked Uncle Otto to pry off the covers. Otto had massive arms and he'd flip off the pot lids as if they were tobacco can tops.

Potted pork liver reminds me of a goose liver pâté. Chop one-and-one-half pounds of unsmoked pork such as fresh bacon, one-and-one-half pounds of shoulder pork and two pounds of pork liver, and season it with five-eighths of a teaspoon of garlic powder, two tablespoons of chopped parsley, a tablespoon of salt and one-eighth teaspoon of white pepper. Thicken with three slightly beaten eggs and four tablespoons of flour. Turn the mixture into greased crocks or one-pound loaf pans which are placed in a larger pan of hot water. Bake at 300° F. for three hours. Cool the potted liver, cover it with melted lard and store in a cool place. To serve, scrape off the lard and slice the meat thin. For buffets or in sandwiches, this pork pot is supreme.

The beauty of having potted foods on hand is the ease with which they may be used. Most potted products need no further cooking and each pot is an individual with its own character and personality. Potted foods are best stored at about 50° F., and should be secured with metal lids to discourage wandering odors and insidious enemies.

Beef is another instant-nourishment pot that produces charitable feelings toward the cook and full bellies for youngsters. Children particularly seem to enjoy this mild, easy-to-chew meat. For potted beef simmer one-and-one-half pounds of soup beef, together with three pork chops and a worn-out ham knuckle. The hambone should not have much meat on it but lots of gelatinous cartilage to make jelly in the pot. Add a stalk or two of chopped celery, an onion, bay leaf, parsley, salt and pepper and cook until the meat falls apart. With a slotted spoon remove the meat, discard any fat and put the meat through the meat chopper. While chopping, boil down the broth by one-half, add a teaspoon of herb bouquet and strain the broth over the chopped meat. Pour the sloppy paste into a sterilized potting crock and slowly oven-bake the beef (250° F.) for one hour. Cool, cover with lard, refrigerate overnight, and for keeping, seal a second time with melted lard.

I have read that beef may be potted in the same manner that Aunt Clair potted scrap pork, but that red wine is preferable to beer. The beef is beaten with a wooden mallet rather than pulled apart, and butter is used as the lubricating agent. The potted beef is sealed with clarified butter and paraffin, lidded and stored in a cool, dark place.

Aunt Clair had a small stone room on one side of the kitchen which she called her still room. There she cured sausages, hung salted pork, started wines, fermented soft beers, brewed, made cheeses and potted foods. She potted cured as well as uncured pork and spiced each pot differently. She believed that potted meat retained moisture and natural flavor better than dry-cured pork. Aunt Clair's crocks of potted meat lined the lower part of her still room; she put rocks on each tin cover to hold them down, and they looked like fat, overcoated soldiers marching along the shelves.

Potting preserves meats that are often scorned. Potting saves pieces which some cooks refuse with contempt. Aunt Clair's potted meats repaid many times their outward value in good eating. All potted foods give abundantly. Like people who exist on the margins of life's mainstreams, a little attention, warmth, and spice, a secure place, do wonders to enhance their worth.

9

Canned

Canning foods, my husband contends, is a symptom of my insecurity. He is correct in that my home canning stems from Depression days, but since then my summer pastime has blossomed into a deeply satisfying ritual. From May, when crimson berries simmer into fragrant jam, until the last golden pears of October settle into their own crystal juice, I am happy canning anything that meanders into my kitchen. True, steaming kettles, heaps of fruit, tedious washing, sorting, chopping, chipping and coring is enough to wilt a woman; but one glimpse of bright home-canned foods holding down a shelf renews the spirit.

Heat is the essential requirement in home canning, because heat destroys bacteria and organisms that cause spoilage and food poisoning. Vacuum sealing of the canning jars further prevents spoilage by inhibiting the entrance of naughty spores. However, vacuum sealing alone does not mean the food is bacteria-free. The deadly *Botulinum clostridium* thrives in airless, sealed jars.

There was a miner near Anchorage, a bony hermit whose brow and jaw seemed clenched into a fist of defense against life, who understood the woes of botulism. He lost a mother-in-law in a rock slide, and while digging out of their marooned mountain valley his wife succumbed to a botulistic ptarmigan. "She insisted with her last breath that the bird, canned by her mother, was good." The miner told me that in settling the estates he discovered that his mother-in-law had also poisoned and buried two husbands with her canned *Botulinum*.

Proper processing and boiling of low-acid foods after opening the jar destroys bacteria. If you are nervous about serving home-canned foods, it is a good rule to boil all vegetables for at least fifteen minutes before tasting.

Utensils needed for home canning are few and inexpensive. A large enamel boiler or canner with a rack and cover is the prime requisite. A jar lifter, colander, hot pot holders, big pots, buckets, a food chopper, knives, spoons and a flat pan in which to sterilize jars. Uncracked and nick-free jars with lids and rings to fit are needed. If low-acid foods are to be canned, a pressure cooker with rack is usually recommended.

Common ways of canning include: (1) boiling-water-bath method; (2) open-kettle method; (3) steam-pressure method; and (4) oven canning.

Unless you are brave around exploding glass and flying fruit, the oven canning method should be discounted.

Although many home-canning activists swear by the steam-pressure method of canning, ever since a bully-type female pedagogue colleague lost a pertinent part of her forward anatomy when her cooker exploded, I stick to the older, slower, more pleasant way of canning. I usually use the boiling-water-bath method. That is, I put the filled and tightly capped jars into a deep kettle, cover them with water and boil them for the prescribed processing time.

For jams and pickling, preserving foods with a high sugar or vinegar content, the open-kettle method of canning is simplest. Put boiling hot produce into hot sterilized jars and seal.

In all canning methods, the jars to be used should be inspected for imperfections, washed, rinsed and sterilized, and left in boiling water until needed.

I wash jars and lids the first thing in the morning on canning day and keep them simmering. If they boil dry, watch out. Melted rubber stinks and is devilish to remove from jars.

The first rule of family canning is to harness all the kid, dog and spouse power you can muster to chop, snap, crack and pop.

Actually the rewards of home canning are far greater than just the visible food in the cellar. Home-grown or self-picked fruits lend individuality to mealtimes. As we suck the sweet, spicy meat from miniature whole-canned pears, we relive the fun we had the day our leader, Lewis, became "momentarily" confused in the woods for a full three hours before leading us to a wild pear tree. We laugh about the fight we had over Martin's giant Siamese-twin yellow tomato. Everyone wanted to eat it on the spot. We finally decided to can it into one quart jar and later divide it into five parts. "Martin's beauty," we called the fruit as we devoured it last winter. Canned berries bring back thoughts of brambles, sticky hot afternoons, then a mini-skinny into the icy spring.

As May days lengthen, harvest and canning time begins. The first rule of putting up food is to relax, enjoy the life; think of how much fine exercise your hands, hips and biceps are getting; let your pores open in the steam of the kitchen and pretend you are rejuvenating your wrinkles in a spa. Relax and think kind thoughts about the fruits of the earth and the goodness of God.

It is important to follow processing directions carefully, because some vegetables contain a high content of starch and will invite bacteria if not properly cooked. Never crowd vegetables in jars because heat cannot penetrate. Do not fill jars level full, because most foods expand with heat and seeds or fibers will collect under the lid. Full jars look great, but unsealed lids are discouraging. Wipe the lip of the jar clean before putting on the lid and ring, checking that the ring is screwed down evenly. Try to pick, pack and process vigorous, young, virgin-type produce the same day.

May is greens time. Mix or match spinach, chard, beet, radish and turnip tops, mustard, kale or wild pot herbs. Add a touch of acid (vinegar) to all greens and "can with a light heart," my grandmother used to say, as she sent me armed with a knife and sack to garden and fields.

Picking over greens is the most important job. Wash, drain, wash a second time, sprinkling the water with salt to settle grit and disgorge sleepy bugs. Trim off stems and discard them with coarse, off-colored leaves. Drain the greens. Cover with boiling water and cook in a large pot until well wilted. Drain, cover with an acid solution made with two cups of 5 percent vinegar to two quarts water. Boil five minutes. Pack the greens loosely in hot, sterilized pint jars. Cut through the greens with a knife, add one-half teaspoon salt and cover with acid liquid to within one inch of the top. Wipe rim clean, put on lid and screw the ring tight. Process pint jars of acid-created greens for sixty minutes in a boiling-water bath. Cool slowly and store.

If you do not care for the flavor of vinegar in greens, or other acid-canned produce, add one-eighth of a teaspoon of baking soda after opening the jar for table use. Do not add soda at the time of canning.

Remember to boil all low-acid foods fifteen minutes before tasting.

Some old timers do not believe in acid canning. They simply pack pre-cooked greens in jars, add one teaspoon salt, seal and process in a boiling-water bath for three hours.

Grandma used her canned greens in Radish Top Soup or in Green Scrapple. Sometimes we ate them simply heated and sprinkled over with a little crisp-fried bacon.

Grandma called her greens soup Radish Top to tease Granddaddy, because he planted radishes only to show where slow-germinating seeds were located, and she would pull them up each year before they had done their job and can them with other greens. Granddaddy would growl, but he loved the soup. Simmer about a pound of lean boiling beef and bone in about two quarts of water, add one-half cup of barley, one cup of stewed tomatoes, pepper and salt to taste. When nearly done, or after about one-and-a-half hours, add a pint of canned and drained greens. Re-cover pot and simmer about one-half hour longer. This thick soup is a hearty meal when served with feather rolls, a salad and burnt sugar cake.

For an oddball icebox meat, my grandmother made Green Scrapple, which I loved with fried apples and mellow baked potatoes. Sauté two cups of lean pork scraps in a little grease. When brown add one cup of tomato purée and a pint of canned drained greens, together with a cup of water, a teaspoon of celery seed, two tablespoons of grated onion, pepper and salt to taste. Cover, simmer for twenty-five minutes, then gradually sprinkle and stir in enough yellow cornmeal to make a thick, plopping mixture. Cook very, very slowly, stirring often, and when almost thick enough to hold the spoon upright, pour into greased molds or bread pans. Cover lightly with waxed paper, cool and refrigerate. The following day, slice, drench with flour and fry.

Rhubarb in May is simple to can, and simply superb to eat later in pies, sauce, tarts, fritters, or, as my grandmother would repeat, "as a cool and pleasing laxative."

Remove leaves and cut rhubarb stalks into one-half-inch lengths. Add one-half cup of sugar to each quart of rhubarb. Let stand for three or four hours to draw out the juice. Bring to a boil, add a pinch of salt, then pack hot into hot sterilized quart jars, seal and process in a boiling-water bath for ten minutes.

On a plateau above Homer, Alaska, where Lewis and I had a homestead and spent our honeymoon (digging two-and-a-half tons of coal), the summer hills flap with big-eared rhubarb. Beautiful country, beautiful honeymoon. To this day Lewis loves rhubarb pie. I thicken a quart of sweetened sauce with two tablespoons of flour, pour it into a crust, daub it with butter, add a top crust, seal, perforate and pop it into an oven, 425° F., for thirty-five minutes. After two or three pieces, Lewis says he is ready to go back to Homer and dig more coal.

Some people add raisins, dates, figs or chopped hickory nuts to rhubarb sauce. Our daughter Penny is crazy about hot rhubarb sauce on fresh corn bread. If I served it three days a week she would lick her chops for more.

Grandma's rhubarb laxative was a favorite in the neighborhood. Squeeze a quart of canned rhubarb through a jelly sack, add a cup of brandy to the heavy, tart liquid and drink a wine glass full before bedtime. I have seen one neighbor sit at the kitchen table and drink four glasses of Grandma's laxative. His constipation must have been severe.

Asparagus is another easy-to-can Maytime sprout. Wash and cut the spears an inch shorter than pint jars. Pre-cook until tender in salted water. Drain. Carefully pack upright into hot jars, add one-half teaspoon salt to each pint and fill to within three-fourths inch of the jar top with boiling acid solution (two cups vinegar to two quarts of water). Seal and process pints for sixty minutes in a boiling-water bath. Cool slowly and store in a dark place.

If you go the non-acid route, process pints of pre-cooked asparagus for three hours in a boiling-water bath.

Canned asparagus should always be handled gently and boiled for fifteen minutes before tasting. Actually, by the time our asparagus is canned and re-cooked, I end up with a purée which can be used in soups and sauces, but canned asparagus does not inspire salad making or the aesthetic senses. My grandmother's canned asparagus was as nondescript as mine, and she usually baked hers into a cheesy casserole.

Strawberries are a May favorite. I generally make jam, wine, brandy or candy from our berries because they seem to lose something in canning, but one year when we were strawberry rich, I canned them to save them. Add one-half cup of sugar to each quart of washed and stemmed berries, and bring them slowly to a boil. Let them stand overnight. Bring the berries quickly to a boil the next morning and pack them hot into hot, sterilized quart jars. Cover them with juice, lid, tighten the rings and process quarts for twenty minutes in a boiling-water bath.

As a breakfast fruit, canned strawberries are good, but of course they cannot be compared to fresh or frozen berries.

My grandmother used to can brandied strawberries and, strewn over ice cream, they were something else! Hull four quarts of berries and heap into a large enamel pan. Add two oranges ground through the medium plate of the food chopper, together with one cup of sugar and one cup of plain brandy. Mix, cover and let stand for four hours. Heat slowly until the sugar dissolves and the berries are hot. Pack hot into sterilized quart jars, seal and process for fifteen minutes in a boiling-water bath.

For years I ate brandied strawberries over hot bread pudding or ice cream and thought that the syrup had been absorbed into the fruit. It was only after I canned brandied strawberries myself that I discovered that somebody had been tapping Grandma's juice. The scarlet liquid is a rich, mellow, fragrant, beautifully smooth brandy.

A nurse friend in Alaska asked if I would live in her house and take care of her dog, turtle, cat, fish and an expensive canary while she visited "outside" for three months. Great! Instant homemaker and all the strawberries I could gorge come Fourth of July.

What a crop! Every raven in the Thlinget nation heard the news and boldly staked claims on my yard. More than once I had to dive for the door to keep from being carried off or pecked to death.

A German neighbor saw my plight and not only mined the area with crow traps (her children, blowing whistles, rode around the patch on their tricycles) but she also gave me a delightful strawberry sherbet recipe that works fine with canned berries.

Mix one package of strawberry gelatin with one-and-one-half cups of sugar and dissolve the mixture in one cup of boiling water. Add the juice of one lemon, cool and stir in one cup of cream and about three-fourths of a quart of canned berries. Pour into a freezer tray and when half-frozen whip with a fork and return to the freezer. Eat this sherbet with its sweet invasion of rosy berries when it is solid.

My nurse friend returned to find everything intact except the empty berry patch and canary. That feathery blonde had flitted out the door when the whistling children were stirring up the neighborhood.

June—the heartbeat of harvesting quickens. Beans, peas, a turnip or two, baby beets, miniature onions, and summer squash beg to be gathered.

Some summer squash, like beautiful women, seem satisfied to contribute color and little else to society or cellars. I have canned yellows and zucchini just to save them, and afterwards I have had to dig up enticing ways with which to enhance their pallid personalities.

To can squash, dice and boil briefly. Drain. Pack hot into hot, sterilized bottles and add one teaspoon of salt to each quart. Cover the squash with boiling vinegar water made by mixing two cups of vinegar with two quarts of water. Seal and boil the jars for one hour in a boiling-water bath.

Our neighbor in Culpeper cans sliced, pre-cooked squash without acid and processes quarts for three hours. To serve, she drains her canned squash, then simmers them with a little butter, sugar and cream until they are almost dry. I have tasted her creamy squash and they are surprisingly good.

Casserole dishes are my answer for the use of mushy canned summer squash. Drain a quart of squash and soak for twenty minutes in fresh water in which a little baking soda has been dissolved. (Mix in only as much soda as will fit on the very tip of your pinky.) Drain, rinse and layer half of the juicy pulp into a greased two-quart casserole. Mix one-half pound of hamburger, one-half cup of raw rice, one tablespoon of olive oil, one small, diced onion, a dash of garlic, parsley, pepper and salt; layer the mixture in the casserole and top with the remaining squash. Daub with butter, salt and pepper, cover with a cabbage leaf or washed grape leaves, lid tightly and bake slowly for one hour. The rice swells, the meat juices weep and squash adds its own bit of prettiness to the dish.

Everyone handles their emptied canning jars a little differently, but they should be washed out immediately after being emptied, then washed in suds and rinsed with the dishes. I pack my clean jars in grocery bags and close the tops so that dust will not infiltrate. My grandmother wrapped each clean jar in newspaper and stored them in bushel baskets. Some people save the boxes in which they were purchased and place the washed bottles upside down in them. One neat housekeeper I know replaces the clean bottles upside down on the shelf for empties. Whatever the *modus operandi*, it is convenient to have your bottles centralized and ready to go at the snatch of a vegetable.

Baby beets not only add color to shelves of canned foods, but when pickled, their flavorful personalities reach out and invite a smile. A neighbor here in suburban Washington told me to plant beets early and to dig them while they are still pups in June. He advised me correctly; I had no luck with beets until I planted and dug early. We eat beet tops cut two inches from the globe as a chard-tasting green, and the infant beets are washed and cooked until tender, slipped from their skins after a plunge in cold water, then trimmed of their tails and crew-cut top-knots. For one gallon of prepared beets, mix four cups of vinegar, two cups of water, two cups of sugar and one-and-one-half teaspoons of salt. Simmer for fifteen minutes with two sticks of cinnamon and one tablespoon of allspice while you pack the beets into sterilized jars. Cover with the boiling liquid and seal. Process these pickled fuchsia babies for thirty minutes in a boiling-water bath.

For the nonvinegar process, the old books say to boil pint jars of baby or cut-up beets in a canner for two hours.

"Little green peas in a pod, taters and catfish: commonly called happiness," our rural delivery postman emoted one June as he popped a packet of seeds into our mailbox, drove down the road with one wheel in the ditch, and waved merrily to all who crossed his vision.

A sociology professor likened prisoners in a cell block to peas in a pod. Plants feel no pain, he said, but human prisoners suffer because imprisonment cuts off acceptable satisfaction of their basic needs: recognition, response, new experience and security.

When I shell peas I cannot help but remember my teacher's words. The peas do not change, nor do released men, my professor lectured. Ex-prisoners seek to satisfy needs and if acceptable means are not available, antisocial ways are sought. The men become repeat offenders.

Canning green peas satisfies a homemaker's basic needs, it is true, but my heart is troubled each June when I remember.

Low-acid foods such as peas require higher processing temperatures to discourage bacteria, and for this reason my grandmother always pre-cooked the peas, canned them in pint jars, processed the jars for three-and-a-half hours in a boiling-water bath, and boiled them for fifteen minutes before serving them. A bushel of peas in the pod will can into twelve or fifteen pints, she told me, as I pumped on the pea sheller and dodged flying peas. Grandma often made a pea soup out of her canned peas by boiling three or four pints with hog hocks, diced potatoes, onion and carrot chips, salt, pepper and water. When everything was mushy, and it seemed that the soup exerted greater effort with each plop, Grandma mashed it through the colander, added boiling water to make it the proper consistency, then served it with a daub of sour cream swimming in the middle of each bowl. A supper of Sneart, as she called the Dutch pea soup, together with Polish Sausage baked in skinny loaves of bread, was great.

Although I tried canning onions the year they developed neck rot and had to be dug prematurely, they turned out to be a wasted effort. Discolored, limp and strong-tasting, my canned onions were not good.

Most fruits contain enough natural acid to be safely canned by the use of the boiling-water-bath method. It is important to use only fresh, firm fruit; overripe or slightly spoiled fruit can turn a whole batch into a punch-happy product.

Fruit may be canned in water, juice or syrup, and my grandmother estimated that about one to one-and-a-half cups of liquid is required for each quart of fruit.

Syrups are sly. If they are too sweet they tend to overpower flavor, if too light they draw the strength from the fruit. Some syrups end up winey (which is not bad, but winey blackberries for your youngsters' breakfasts might give pause to those they breathe on in school). Some syrup goes the whole route and turns into vinegar. And I made one batch of syrup with honey that tasted like thyme or sage.

LIQUIDS FOR CANNING FRUIT

Light syrup . . . one cup of sugar dissolved by boiling in three cups of water or juice.

Medium syrup . . . one cup of sugar dissolved by boiling in two cups of water or juice.

Heavy syrup . . . one cup of sugar dissolved by boiling in one cup of water or juice.

Honey may be substituted for one-third of the sugar if you wish a medium syrup, or replace sugar with honey, cup for cup, if you wish a light syrup. I sometimes substitute brown sugar for white if I desire a more rich, but not necessarily a sweeter syrup. Generally speaking, I can fruit using the light syrup, or plain, unsweetened juice.

Creatures and man seem to vie for the honor of possessing the most patience during June while waiting for raspberries, mulberries and cherries to redden. Bugs, birds and boys eye the fruit, test, taste, then step back to wait. At the first signal that the fruit is ripe, the grand scramble is on.

To can mulberries I pack ripe and unripe, washed but unstemmed berries into hot sterilized jars, cover with a boiling light syrup, seal and process in a boiling-water bath for thirty minutes. Then on a windy wintry day I open the jars, strain the mulberries through a cheesecloth and, using an equal amount of sugar and the juice of one lemon per quart, I boil the mauve liquid into a cloudy jelly. It has a musty taste, like a warm-damp wine cellar.

After butchering time early each winter, my grandmother used to serve mulberry jelly with a dish she called German Pork Chops. Dip six or eight lean chops in flour, sprinkle with pepper and salt and fry brown in butter. Lay each brunette chop in a heavy pot, top each with a thick slice of lemon and a teaspoon of mulberry jelly. Wash out the frying pan with one-half cup of water and pour over the chops. Cover the pot tightly and simmer for one-and-one-half hours. Carefully remove the meat, add water to the drippings and thicken the tangy, honey-like gravy with flour. Serve with mashed potatoes, corn fritters and hot gingerbread. My grandfather used to smear mulberry jelly on his chops, fritters and gingerbread, but that was too much for me; German Pork Chops are succulently sweet and superb just as they come out of the pot.

Raspberries tend to mush when heated but their soft dispositions do not alter their intense flavor. I use canned berries in an icebox dessert that takes five minutes to make and less time for our family to eat. Mix one cup of sugar, a cup or so of drained berries, one-half cup orange juice and a tablespoon of lemon juice in a bowl. Add about one-and-one-half cups of milk and one cup of cream. (I use evaporated milk.) Pour into a refrigerator tray. Set freezer at the coldest level, stir twice at ten-minute intervals, then return the control to its regular place until table time.

To can raspberries pack the washed, raw fruit into hot sterilized quart jars, shake down for a closer pack and fill the jar to within an inch of the top with a boiling medium or light syrup. Seal. Process twenty minutes in a boiling-water bath.

Cherries may be canned with or without pits. Grandma used to put me on the business end of the pitter when she canned pitless pie cherries in light syrup. She mixed one-half cup sugar to each quart of pitted cherries, heated them slowly until hot through, then packed them into hot sterilized quart jars. She covered the cherries with syrup if they had not made enough of their own juice, sealed the jars and processed each quart for fifteen minutes in a boiling-water bath.

In addition to plain two-crusted pie, cherries may be made into a sour cream pie. Line a pie pan with crust, pour in one quart of well-drained, semi-sweetened cherries. Mix in a bowl one cup sour cream, one-half cup brown sugar, a pinch of salt and a tablespoon of flour. Pour over the cherries and bake at 425° F. for twenty minutes or until golden.

July turns garden gathering into urgent happiness. My mail carrier used to say that people of limited intelligence are happier. Clever people are far less happy, he added, because the worm of doubt gnaws. I must be endowed with the limited variety of intelligence because come bean and berry time, I am my happiest self.

Canned beans and berries seem to give the greatest benefits for the teeniest efforts. A bushel of beans will can into about twenty quarts and a quart of berries yields about a quart of fruit. I do not pack either food tightly in their jars because we love to drink berry juice, and with the beans, heat must penetrate into the center of each jar to destroy bacteria.

On bean-canning days I wash, rinse and sterilize jars and lids; pick, trim, snap and wash green or wax beans. Actually the whole family helps to pick and snap, then I boil the beans for ten minutes, pack them hot into sterilized quart jars, add one teaspoon salt to each quart and cover the beans with the water in which they had been boiled. I wipe the lips of the jars, fasten each lid tightly and transfer the jars to the rack in the canner. I process quarts of wax or green beans for three hours in a boiling-water bath.

It is important to have the temperature of the canner water approximately the same as that of the jars. When jars fill the canner space without crowding or tipping, I fill the kettle with hot water to cover the jars, put the lid on and process. When opened in winter, season the beans with bacon and onion or butter, then heat, eat and enjoy the rewards of July.

Blackberries are as simple to put up as beans. First, get your loving husband or friendly neighbor to help you pick. Allow an hour of picking time to the quart, so that you can get in lots of good conversation over the berry bushes. Promise him a cobbler, pie, wine by candlelight, anything. Picking berries by yourself is just no fun.

Back home, wash, pick over (anything that moves, discard), drain, measure berries and put them into a large pot. Add one-quarter to one-half cup of sugar for each quart, stir and mash them until a bit of juice forms, then heat slowly until the berries turn an exquisite red and they come to a boil. Spoon them into sterilized quarts, add boiling water or juice to cover, wipe the jar lips clean, seal and process in a boiling-water bath for fifteen minutes.

Over ice cream, for breakfast, in pies and puddings, canned blackberries go over big with all who do not have false teeth. If someone in your family wears dentures, it is simple enough to put the berries through a sieve when you open the jar and use the berry mush in a full-bodied pie. Someday I am going to try canning seedless berries because they make a surprisingly delicious sauce.

In Alaska I helped can huckleberries by packing one quart of washed berries into sterilized jars in alternating layers with one-half cup of sugar. The quarts were shaken to settle the fruit, then lidded, sealed and processed in a boiling-water bath for twenty minutes. They were always a favorite. I even made a latter-day wine out of canned blueberries. Tasted good, but turned my guests' teeth green.

Huckleberry pudding turns nothing green except your girlfriends who are competing with you for the attention of local bachelors.

Soak eight slices of dry bread in two cups of milk and mash in one quart of canned and drained blueberries or hucks. Beat in two eggs, a half teaspoon of salt, a tablespoon of sugar and a little vanilla. Watch your competitors bow at your altar!

This recipe was given to me by a buxom cook who knew all about altars. She was on her sixth or seventh husband, and each of them had given her a diamond that would choke a hen.

"Berries and beans, corn and fish, and one year cantaloupe," my grandmother would answer when asked what she canned in July. The canning of corn is not generally recommended with the boiling-water bath because this method does not supply enough heat to destroy the bacteria that spoil starchy vegetables. Some of the old-timers had luck canning corn in pints and processing them for three-and-a-half hours, but Grandma's plain canned corn always went to ferment, so she salt-canned it.

Cut plump corn from the cob and measure. For every nine cups of corn add two cups of water and one cup of salt. Boil for twenty minutes, stirring constantly. Pack boiling corn into hot sterilized pint jars, seal and process sixty minutes in a boiling-water bath. When opened for use, rinse in water, then parboil the corn for thirty minutes in fresh water to remove the salt. To serve, Grandma drained the freshened corn, sprinkled it with a bit of sugar, flavored it with a lump of butter, pepper and sometimes a quarter-cup or so of thick cream. With a dinner of mincemeat-stuffed pork roast, scalloped potatoes and stewed fruit, canned corn can't be beat.

On muggy hot July days, when the moon was wet and new, my grandfather loved to sneak through early morning mists and fish in the lazy, mirror-still creeks near St. Joseph, Missouri. Sometimes he would take me with him. Granddaddy usually cleaned his fish on the creek bank, but later when the sun burned hot we returned home, and he finished scaling, removing fins and washing the fish in the chicken yard before he brought his catch to the kitchen. We often had a mess of crisp fried fish right then. Afterward, if Grandma's frugal Swiss blood got the best of her, she would can the surplus.

To can fine-boned fish such as log perch, cut the fish into pieces an inch short of the length of a pint jar; submerge and soak them for one hour in a brine made of one-half pound salt to one gallon of water. Drain the fish in a colander for ten minutes, then bring them to a boil in a vinegar-water solution made of two parts vinegar and one part water. Drain and immediately pack the hot fish, skin side out, into hot sterilized pint jars. Fill to cover the fish with fresh, regular vinegar water (two cups vinegar to two quarts water) that has been previously boiled with spices, horseradish root and pepper pods. Wipe the jar lips and seal. Process pints for four hours in a boiling-water bath.

Grandma emphasized that home-canned "Winegar fish," as she called them, could not be eaten or even tasted until after they had been thoroughly cooked. She usually prepared canned fish into a zesty fish loaf, which we ate nearly every Friday night from December until Lent.

The one time Grandma canned cantaloupe occurred when a train derailed and spilled a boxcar of melons on Uncle Otto's crossing. As we returned from the track-side harvest, Grandma declared that she would save the juicy fruit.

After seeding, scooping and spooning the centers of hundreds of melons into an enormous pile, she fed them into the food chopper, then boiled the honey-orange mass with half its volume of sugar and one-half dozen ground lemons. Over low fires and occupying every pan and pot in the house, the cantaloupe mush boiled all day and all night. The air for blocks around was heavy with the sickening aroma of boiled cantaloupe. Bees swarmed. Flies lined the screens. Yellow jackets dug an emergency nest in the carnation bed adjacent to the kitchen door.

When we threw out the cantaloupe concoction, even the chickens would not eat it.

But as the saying goes, it's a long lane that has no turning. It turned out that the insects flocked to the chicken yard, where our hens got fat on bug juice.

August makes an honest woman of me. As home canning revs to takeoff speed, my spirit becomes airborne and I glory in the abundance of produce to put up.

I start with applesauce. There are two main ways of preparing apples: peel, quarter and core, or quarter, core, cook and press the apples through a sieve.

I prefer to wash apples (a variety that will mush well when cooked), then peel, quarter and core them before cooking in a little water. This method seems to go more pleasantly than mashing hot apples through a food mill or colander. I usually pick out a good T.V. show, put my apples in front of me and peel like hell. I pared, quartered and cored a bushel during one Edward G. Robinson epic last year, and the bad guys really got it from my knife. I cut, stabbed, sliced and poked apples as I became involved. Great therapy. Some authorities advise soaking the peeled apples in salted vinegar water (two tablespoons each to a gallon of water) to prevent darkening, but if you peel fast the apples will stay bright.

After the apples are peeled, I boil or steam them with a little water in a large covered pan, and when they are mushy I add approximately one-quarter cup of sugar and a pinch of salt to each quart of sauce. I spoon the boiling hot fruit into hot sterilized jars, wipe the rim clean with a paper towel that has been dipped into boiling water, and seal. Quarts of applesauce are processed for fifteen minutes in a boiling-water bath. My canner holds about ten or eleven quarts; a bushel of apples cans into about fifteen quarts of sauce, so with perseverance and a couple of good T.V. movies, I am able to put up about thirty quarts of applesauce in a day. About fifty or sixty quarts keeps our family of five in applesauce for a year.

Some years I can firm apples for use in winter pies and employ the same method, but the apples end up chunky and a bit more tart than applesauce.

Gooseberries or wild currants can beautifully. Wash, snip tails, boil the berries briefly with a little water and a pinch of baking soda, add one-half to three-fourths cup of sugar for each quart of fruit, boil until the sugar is dissolved, then fill hot sterilized jars with the hot berries and juice. Wipe the jar lips, seal and process for twenty minutes in a boiling-water bath.

Pied or sauced, or oozing from the edges of Banbury tarts,

gooseberries are one of the earth's grand gifts for those who enjoy living off the land and preserving its goodness.

Hot August days and brisk nights bring out the pungent gypsyness of elderberries and their fruit heads bow, begging to be picked. My grandparents used to put down crocks of berries in vinegar and sugar, but each summer I can a few quarts for pie filling. I add one tablespoon of vinegar to each quart of elderberries after the washed, stemmed and slightly mashed fruit has been brought to a boil in a light syrup. I then spoon the berries and juice into sterilized jars, seal and process for twenty minutes in a boiling-water bath.

I once met a Gypsy who believed in the potency of elderberries. He claimed an elixir of *Sambucus* would clear the head, cure a cold, and that its consumption endowed a person with unnatural perception. He said that his distilled product was better than a truth serum if taken by the proper people. He vowed that his elder-triggered psychic vibrations had led him across the country, through New York City and south to Florida the summer that his wife ran off with a Cuban. The Gypsy's wife, a bony blonde, agreed that the power of the elder was mystical, but added that their elderberry potion did not help her find her foster son whom, she said, she was seeking when her husband apprehended her in Florida.

Sambucus, sambuca, psychic serum or not, plain old-fashioned Midnight Elder Pie made from canned berries, is wonderful.

With peaches and plums, the high point of preserving arrives in our house. Wash full, ripe, but still firm peaches, blanch in boiling water for two minutes to loosen skins, then dip into cold water, drain and slip skins. Cut away discolored areas, split peaches into halves, and pit. Drop the skinned peach halves into hot sterilized quart jars and cover with boiling syrup. Wipe lips of the jars and seal. Process quarts of peaches for thirty minutes in a boiling-water bath.

"The impudence of simplicity! Confidence of the stupid!" my grandmother would mutter if she were here now and saw me loading jars with such carefree abandon. My grandmother handled every peach with tender loving care and packed perfect halves in manicured layers, cavity side down. Today, however, time dictates that we all pop and run; I am not as neat as my grandmother.

A breeze
Helps bees
Pollinate trees
To set a crop of plums.

Thick-skinned, sour, juicy Americans: the wild goose, chicka-
saw, Canada and black sloe plums were all canned by pioneer
mothers. Today's mothers fancy the French and green gage
plums for their sweetmeats. Plums, either wild or commercial,
are neither peeled nor pitted; they have only to be pricked to
prevent bursting, washed, heated and canned in syrup.

Layer plums two deep in a flat pan, cover them with boiling
medium syrup, lid the pan and let the plums absorb heat for
thirty minutes before packing them into sterilized jars. After removing the plums from the flat pan, reheat the syrup, fill the
jars with the boiling liquid, seal and process quart jars for twenty
minutes in a boiling-water bath.

Our family prefers canned plums served whole in sauce dishes
so that we can see if anyone gets a slit seed (a good luck sign).
But canned fruits add personality to kuchen, batter pudding,
and they are delicious in dumplings on a windy wet night.

Apricots, nectarines, ripe grapes and figs all may be canned
with ease and safety by packing the prepared fruit with hot
syrup and processing in a boiling-water bath. No extensive or
expensive equipment is needed, no great technical know-how is
required. The ritual of home canning in August is a natural response to the urgencies of shorter days and harvest.

September, the time has come to can tomatoes. Overripe fruit
odors, rag pollen, musky weeds, dry grassy smells fill the garden square. Insect hums are stilled as eggs are laid and cocoons
perfected. Scarlets, pinks, claret reds and golden globes compete
for brilliance under tired vines. Tomatoes are ripe.

Wash firm, ripe tomatoes, blanch in boiling water, then dip
quickly into a cold bath. Slip skins, core, and for cold-pack tomatoes, drop the fruit into hot sterilized quarts, add one teaspoon salt and cover with juice or boiling water. Cut through
the tomatoes with a knife, wipe the lips of the jars clean and
seal. Process cold-pack or raw-pack quarts forty-five minutes in
a boiling-water bath.

Hot-pack tomatoes are briefly boiled in a large kettle after
their skins and cores are removed. The boiling fluid and fruit

are ladled into hot sterilized jars, one teaspoon of salt is added to each quart, the jar lips are wiped and the jars are sealed. Process hot-pack tomatoes for fifteen minutes in a boiling-water bath.

Tomato juice is made by simmering ripe tomatoes until soft, then pressing the fruit through a sieve. Bring the juice just to a boil, mix in one teaspoon sugar and one teaspoon salt per quart and pour the hot juice into hot sterilized jars. Wipe the rims, seal and process in a boiling-water bath for fifteen minutes.

Tomato paste and tomato purée are made similarly to juice, but the tomato pulp is cooked until it is thick before seasoning and canning. Beware of burned purée. I scorched a boiler of strained tomatoes one year, then was dumb enough to can it. Every time I reached for a quart of purée I grabbed one of my burned triumphs; I could not tell the good jars from the ones with "poor man's flavoring" until they were opened.

Pizza sauce, cocktail juice, tomatoes stewed with onions and peppers, okra and eggplant with tomatoes, relishes and succotash: the variety of tomato preserves are endless, but you must put up six or eight quarts of green tomato mincemeat and several jars of green tomato slices for frying before frost closes down your garden for the winter.

To can green tomatoes, wash and cut into one-half inch slices. Sprinkle with one teaspoon of salt to each quart of fruit and let stand for an hour. Drain, pack into quart jars and cover with boiling water. Add one teaspoon of salt and one tablespoon of vinegar to each jar, wipe the jar lips, lid, seal and process for twenty minutes in a boiling-water bath.

Sometimes when I've spent the day out of the house, shopping, browsing in a used-book store, or just "playing with the girls," and I rush home thirty minutes before suppertime, zippity zap! it's fried green tomatoes and sausage gravy. My family dives in while I chatter about my adventures in the new world of people. They love Mom to take a day off, because everything seems topsy-turvy and the house takes on a sort of disorganized glow of impetuosity.

For fried green tomatoes and sausage gravy, crumble about a cup of bulk sausage in the skillet, lid the pan and fry (stirring once or twice) for about ten minutes. While the meat is cooking dash to the basement, snatch a can of green tomatoes, drain them and on a sheet of wax paper mix a dressing of two tablespoons of flour with two tablespoons of cornmeal. When the sausage is done, remove the meat with a slotted spoon, pour off part of the grease and put the skillet back on the fire. Dredge the tomatoes in the flour mixture and fry them, three or four minutes on each side, or until crisp and brown. Layer the tomatoes in a deep platter and keep them warm while you make a cream gravy out of two tablespoons of flour swished with a fork into two tablespoons of drippings and lightened with two cups of milk. Salt and pepper to taste, and when the gravy is thick, add the sausage to it, boil for three minutes and pour over the sliced tomatoes. Plop some sour cream on the top, if you have it, and garnish with a bit of paprika. Serve immediately over toast. With wedges of cold fruit, a leftover dessert and a bowl of peanuts to munch on, this is a happy-go-lucky supper.

Home canning tapers off in October. Pears, persimmons and cranberries may be preserved in their own juice. If you have late carrots or limas, celery or salsify, they may be saved by using the acid-canning technique (two cups vinegar to two quarts water) and processing them in a boiling-water bath for one hour.

Pears are the only fruit that I regularly can during October. We found a fat Bartlett pear tree on our place in the country one year and watched it covetously for the ripening of its fruit. Wild or escaped fruit trees should be spotted in April or May when they bloom, or find fruit trees the hard way by following game trails when deer and lesser animals feast on the fruit. (I followed a well-worn trail one time and ended up at a still. The mash smelled great but I got prickles on the back of my neck and left the glen without looking back. Game trails are not always to be trusted.)

Pears should be picked when mature, then kept in a cool place to ripen. When golden but not mushy, I peel, quarter and core our pears, boil them until tender, drain them, pack them into sterilized quart jars and cover the pears with a light syrup. I fill each jar to within one inch of the top, wipe the jar rim and seal. Quarts are processed thirty minutes in a boiling-water bath. By the time October rolls around I usually have used all my jars except oddballs and half-gallons. Because we enjoy pears for breakfast, for salads and as a clean, light dessert, I often can them in half-gallon jars. For two-quart containers, increase the processing time in the boiling-water bath by one-half.

I often think of the quiet vegetable world when I am canning in the steaminess of my kitchen. I ponder over the invisible principles of all life, and like Linnaeus, I bow my head in worship.

May to October, the year brings hope in growing things and the inherent hope of canning and saving the surplus. With hope there is faith, a faith in God and in the goodness of our earth.

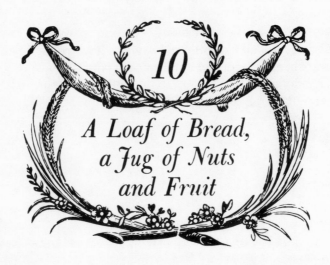

10

A Loaf of Bread, a Jug of Nuts and Fruit

I have a friend who, when her teen-agers were traversing their scatter-brained phase, triumphed over disorganization by regularly making bread. Even though her husband earned a fortune and her social obligations were demanding, she preserved her bi-weekly baking schedule.

"Why?" I asked.

Smiling with all the charm and freshness of a happy high school girl, she answered directly, "Joy."

Some would belittle my friend, saying that fools and children are easily made happy. Others would wistfully observe that happiness, the acceptance of happiness, is the rarest of blessings.

Baking bread is a blessing.

Working warm, pliant dough is physically satisfying. Creating a useful product is psychologically rewarding. Bread making, like gardening, brewing, fermenting, pickling, and canning and curing, supports a faith in the future.

I try to bake every Monday, and although I am not as regular as my "joy" friend, I get kicks from dough, too.

Needs for home bread baking are simple: bowl, spoon, pans, willing biceps and a hot oven.

The basic ingredient of light bread is flour. The most widely used flour is made from wheat—either from the inner part of the grain, which makes white flour, or from the whole grain.

A Loaf of Bread, a Jug of Nuts and Fruit

Wheat contains a protein that combines with moisture to form gluten, a grayish substance that gives elasticity to dough. As yeast ferments, wheat dough expands and holds gas bubbles; thus it becomes "light."

Hard wheats, grown principally north and west of Missouri, are considered better for bread baking because they contain extra gluten. Soft wheats, grown in more humid areas, contain greater amounts of starch and are recommended for cakes. All-purpose flour is made up of specific ratios of gluten and starch.

If flour was unmarked, my grandmother would take a pinch of it between her forefinger and thumb and rub lightly. Hard wheat flour was gritty; soft wheat flour was velvet-smooth, she said.

In bread-making qualities, rye flour resembles wheat flour but is less elastic. Dark rye flour contains some of the outer parts of the grain while light rye is usually the inner part. Straight-grade rye flour normally consists of 30 percent dark flour and 70 percent light.

Bean flours are made by grinding the whole bean or only the inner part and contain more protein than wheat but they require the addition of wheat flour for gluten. The usual proportions are four of wheat flour to one of bean. Soybean flours have higher nutritive quality than other bean flours. They contain less starch and thus are used in smaller quantities in combination with wheat flour: usually five parts of wheat to one of soybean.

Yeasts, like other hothouse plants, thrive in cozy places. Dry granular yeast requires no special storage to insure freshness, and I find dry yeast simple to use. Cake yeast makes equally good bread, but must be stored in the refrigerator.

I once made light bread from the same sourdough starter for a year, and this liquid yeast actually became possessive. If I didn't use it and reactivate its life, it fumed and smelled vile. My sourdough became so dominant that I dared not ignore its demands. I baked whether we needed bread or not. I baked because my sourdough raved and raised its pockmarked head above the jar and ran over the shelf if I did not obey and take some of its goo and give it nourishment. Gradually, I woke up to the fact that my sourdough was worse than a spoiled brat. With that realization, I walked out of the kitchen and left it.

Three weeks later, when we returned from vacation, my

starter was dead. It had rallied for one final blow, however. Some time later, when Lewis wanted to put down new floor tile, he couldn't budge the cabinet. We had named the sourdough starter Old Chris after a real sourdough on the Yukon who tried to court me and, when I refused to wed, promptly died and left fifty thousand dollars to his dog. Like that character, our Old Chris also possessed a vindictive streak. He had glued the cabinet to the floor so tight that Lewis tore off the bottom when he finally broke it loose. Since then, I've never really trusted sourdoughs.

While visiting the Pioneers' Home in Sitka, I discovered that Alaskans coveted their sourdough with passionate possessiveness. One old-timer whose starter "bred true" for forty-five years chased a man who stole his sourdough and lost his leg in the fight. "But I got my starter back and I'm going to be all right," he added firmly. "You get to know and love your sourdough like your dog . . . valuable as a good dog."

"Worth more than most women," a disillusioned codger yelled from across the room.

The clamor of a Bartok symphony is peaceful compared with the shouting on that ward in the Pioneers' Home when I asked the best way to make sourdough bread. I ran for an attendant.

A synopsis of opinion seemed to be that most men dumped their starter into a pan of lukewarm water, added salt, a little grease and sugar if they had it, and flour to thicken "like paste." The men let their dough set in a warm place while they "done the chores," and when the sourdough was activated they saved a chunk the size of a baseball for their starter jar, then flattened patties on a flour surface. Most of the Alaskan Pioneers baked their bread on a hot stove lid. Nostalgia hung heavy in the bright room when I left. My heart went out to the old men, and at home my girlfriend and I spent the night making light bread that we brought to the ward on the way to church the next morning. The Pioneers were polite, smacked their gums, grinned, but one brave soul observed, "Warn't sourdough, but pretty good for a woman."

Sourdough makes lively pancakes and pastry with a hairy personality, but it is an unpredictable friend. If you dare to create a sourdough starter, dissolve one package of dry yeast in a cup of warm water and stir in one teaspoon of sugar. Mix in two-thirds of a cup of flour, cover and keep at room temperature for three or four days. Stir it down and sprinkle with flour from time to time, and when it is well established cover it lightly and store in a cool place until ready to use. The night before you plan to bake with sourdough, mix a little flour, sugar and warm water into the starter and set it in a warm place. The next morning reserve one part of the sourdough starter for future use and mix the other half into hot cake batter, bread dough or pastry-like rolls.

I have heard that sourdough flavor may be infiltrated into bread by the use of old dough that has been allowed to turn sour and harden. A friend from Nenana reserves an egg-sized piece of bread dough, puts it into a cup, lets it rise and turn brown and hard and when she wishes to make a new batch of bread she soaks her wad of soured dough in warm water and crumbles it into her regular yeast bread recipe. I did not stay until her bread was baked, but the odor of the rising dough was sour.

Besides flour and yeast, the basic ingredients of bread are liquid (beer, milk, old potato water), sugar, salt and fat.

Regardless of the ingredients there are two standard methods of making light bread: (1) straight dough method; (2) sponge method.

For a batch of four one-pound loaves of white bread using the straight dough method, dissolve one package of dry yeast in a cup of lukewarm water, add one teaspoon of sugar, stir and let stand for five minutes; or use one cup of liquid starter. When the yeast has done its thing and the surface of the liquid is loaded with ecru bubbles, add three cups more liquid (room temperature) and stir in four teaspoons of salt, four tablespoons of sugar and four tablespoons of melted shortening. When dissolved and well mixed, start adding flour. Twelve scant cups of flour, more or less, will be needed. The initial mixing of the flour with the liquid is the only icky step in bread making.

The dough becomes stiff and sticky, glutinous and unpretty. Perseverance will triumph, and as soon as the mass hangs together, dump it on a floured surface, flour your hands abundantly and knead the gucky dough. Gradually a firm ball will form; then working with the warm, elastic dough becomes a joy. Knead until smooth, or until, as my grandmother would say, "It has a sheen like a baby's bare behind."

Put the dough back into the bowl, grease it, cover with a lid and place it in a warm spot. In cold weather some farm wives let their bread rise over a pan of warm water. I set my bowl close to the pilot on the gas stove. When double in bulk, punch the dough down either on the floured kneading surface or in the bowl. This second brief kneading lets out some of the gas so that fermentation can continue without stretching the elasticity of the gluten too far and injuring the dough.

Let the dough rise a second time to about double its volume, then turn it on a board, divide it into loaf-sized portions, cover and let it stand a few minutes to seal over surfaces.

Mold each into a loaf with the sealed edges down. Place in a greased pan and lightly grease the top surface for the last rising. Let the loaves rise until doubled and bake at around 400° F. for about forty minutes.

Most bakers who use the sponge method of bread making start the sponge the evening before they wish to bake. The same ingredients: yeast, sugar, salt, shortening and part of the liquid and flour are mixed to form a soft spongy dough that is covered and left to rise overnight in a draft-free place. The following morning, more liquid and flour are added to make a medium-firm dough, then kneaded and placed in a bowl, greased, covered and left to rise until double in bulk. The dough is then handled in the same manner as the straight dough method of making bread.

If you prefer to use a yeast starter such as sourdough instead of commercial yeast, the starter should be activated with warm water, flour and a teaspoon of sugar prior to making bread. If you use your starter every day, the activation period will be short; if you bake with your starter every week or two, the starter should be given a boost to produce the night before making bread. It is important to save a cup of your starter each time.

Light rolls are made by the same general methods as loaf breads. They usually contain a little more sugar or fat, and milk is recommended as the liquid ingredient because milk makes a softer product. I usually add two room-temperature eggs to the light roll dough, too; eggs give color and gloss, and glossy rolls add a festive touch to supper.

Dried fruits may be soaked, chopped and added to a portion of dough for breakfast bread or buns. At the first mixing I add about one-half cup fruit (or jam that is not too juicy) to one loaf-sized hunk of dough, then let the dough rise and bake it along with the main batch. After I take the bread from the oven, I ice the hot loaf with powdered sugar, butter, vanilla or rum flavoring. The hot bread will melt the icing so it will be shiny and pretty when it dries.

For nut bread I add one-half cup of chopped hickory or walnuts to a loaf-sized portion of the dough at the first mix. I also increase the sugar in the nut bread at that time by gradually sprinkling two additional teaspoons of sugar into the wad of dough. Be careful to remove all the walnut shells. One year a fireman, Granddaddy's co-worker, snitched a piece of nut bread that Grandma had sent to the station for my grandfather's lunch. A nut shell broke the thief's upper plate, one-half of the denture lodged crosswise in his mouth and he had to ride six miles to the dentist with his mouth open.

Peanut butter bread does not turn me on, but my children beg for a loaf from time to time. At the first mixing I add one-half cup of crunchy peanut butter to a loaf-sized portion of dough and increase the sugar by two teaspoons. I knead the peanut butter and sugar into the dough and proceed as for white bread. Toasted, peanut butter bread is not bad, but plain, it just lies there.

I have put one cup of finely chopped onions in a loaf-sized lump of dough at the first mixing, then rolled the loaf in chopped onion after the second kneading before putting the loaf in a pan.

Drained, finely chopped ripe olives in plain bread dough makes an interesting loaf.

There is no end to the variety of life if you have the dough.

Lewis enjoys a loaf of cheese bread, or a pan of cheese light rolls. Again, I add one-half cup of coarsely grated cheddar cheese to a loaf-sized wad of white bread dough at the first mixing, but I do not add more sugar. Recently I crumbled blue cheese into a bit of plain dough for a pan of rolls; they were superb. With a supper of potato soup, celery sticks and mince pie, blue cheese rolls go great! Commercial grated cheese, such as Parmesan, does not do much for bread. In fact, when I tried it, Lewis asked why I had put sawdust in the dough. It's moments like that when nostalgic thoughts of sweet spinsterhood take over my fuzzy married brain; on the other hand, I remember early efforts with ropy bread that my indulgent groom lumped down and pronounced "interesting" with a smile of encouragement.

Cinnamon rolls or sticky buns are always fun, and go over

"like *big*" with young people. Just last week our seventeen-year-old came home from school and devoured a nine-inch cake pan full of sticky rolls made with peach preserves and swizzles of honey. Like most growing boys he was ready to eat supper two hours later.

I usually save a wad of twice-risen straight bread dough for sweet rolls or pizza. If I am short on time I profusely butter the portion to be saved and store the dough in a plastic wrapper in the icebox. About two hours before roll-out time, I take the dough from the refrigerator to rise. Bread dough seems to handle more easily after a day or two or even a week in cold storage.

For cinnamon buns, roll the room-temperature dough about one-quarter inch thick. Spread with butter, cinnamon, sugar and raisins (or nuts or jam). Beginning with the side of the dough closest to you, roll it up as you would a jelly roll. Pull the remaining edge across the dough and seal with water. Cut into one-half-inch slices, place closely together on a buttered cake tin and dot with butter. Let the rolls rise to double their bulk and bake at 400° F. for fifteen or twenty minutes.

When done remove from the pan and ice immediately with confectioner's sugar mixed into a stiff paste with vanilla and dab of butter. Butter mellows the sugar icing and inhibits cracking.

Young and svelte, old and ordinary folks, all love homemade cinnamon rolls. I know an old-maid-type, forty-one-year-old librarian who literally rolled her way into an Army major's heart with cinnamons and stickies. We shared an apartment and I knew how she often spent half the night putting down dough for her swain's hot breakfast rolls. They are married now and live in the Keys. I have always meant to inquire if she still makes bread at night.

For Sticky Buns, I substitute nuts for raisins. I proceed as for making cinnamon rolls, but about five minutes before the buns are to come out of the oven, I drizzle honey over the nearly baked rolls. I pop the pan back into the oven and bake until all the syrup runs together and the buns are sitting fat and happy in bubbly, brown juice.

Remember to remove the sticky buns from the pan of buns and with one quick motion turn the whole thing upside down.

Eaten at once, they are terrific. Eaten later, they are undoubtedly equally terrific, but I never have any left to cool.

Oddball breads are a welcome change to most families, and

Potato Bread is a primitive loaf that possesses a wine-like flavor. In 1936 we had a magnificent potato crop and Grandma used potatoes for everything: body power, wallpaper paste, stain remover, floor polish and bread. For this no-yeast bread, peel a medium potato and slice it thinly into one quart of boiling water that has been removed from the fire. Add one tablespoon each of sugar and salt, and two tablespoons of cornmeal. Stir the mixture well and keep it lukewarm for a day or two or until it begins to "work" or smell fermented.

Remove the potatoes, add one cup of warm milk and enough flour to make a sponge. Cover and let rise in a warm place (80° to 86° F.) overnight.

The following morning stir in two more cups of warm water, one-half cup each of sugar and shortening and a teaspoon of salt. Knead in enough flour to make a good dough, shape and put into greased pans and let rise until double in size. My grandmother baked Potato Bread at 375° F. for forty minutes and said that the trick to this recipe was to keep the dough warm (80° to 86° F.) at all times.

I once read in an old Ag book that sweet potato flour was manufactured in the 1870's, and a neighboring farm wife told me that Sweet Potato Bread has been made by their family since the Civil War when their other crops were ravaged by repeated skirmishes across their land. Her old uncle, an enormous man with an enormous memory for detail, told us about Jackson "suppering" with them on sweet 'tater bread, apples and side meat. He related his memories of Jackson pacing the floor, then kneeling to pray for an hour before he went to sleep. The uncle was a little boy at that time and his biggest wish was that the war would last long enough for him to join Jackson.

For Sweet Potato Bread the lady told me to peel, boil and mash five large sweet potatoes. Cool one cup of the sweet potato water to lukewarm and in it dissolve one package of dry yeast. While the yeast is activating, mix two eggs, two tablespoons of lard and two teaspoons of salt into the potatoes, then add the liquid yeast and mix well. Gradually stir in flour to make a dough and knead for ten minutes. Grease the top cover and let the dough rise in a draft-free place overnight. The next morning poke down, form into loaves or biscuits and when double in size bake in a quick oven (425° F.) for thirty to forty-five minutes.

Flours made from cracked grains and meals have less baking strength than white flour and for best results should be used with wheat flour.

For oatmeal bread, mix three cups of finely ground rolled oats with about nine cups of all-purpose flour. Reduce the fat to two tablespoons and proceed as for white bread, straight dough method.

Soybean bread requires two cups of sifted soybean flour mixed with about ten-and-a-half cups of white flour and a reduction of the fat to two tablespoons. Proceed as for white bread, straight dough method.

I sometimes use one-half whole wheat flour in my regular straight dough bread, and sometimes my family enjoys a Molasses Wheat. Scald one cup of milk and combine with one-third cup of molasses, one-and-one-half teaspoons of salt and three tablespoons of melted shortening. Cool to lukewarm and add one egg, one package of dry yeast that has been dissolved in a cup of warm water and two-and-one-half cups each of whole wheat and white flour. Knead, and add more flour if necessary. When satiny, grease top and put in a bowl to rise in a warm place. When double in bulk, poke down and let rise a second time. Knead briefly, shape and let rise in pans. Bake at 400° F. for forty minutes. Though wheat breads are lazy and sit heavy in the pans, they are tempting when toasted for breakfast and served with sweet butter, or for luncheon schmiered with Schmierkase.

Beer Bread is popular in our house—after one slice your muscles explode with vitality. Uncap a quart of dark beer, let it go dead and heat the brew to lukewarm together with three tablespoons of molasses. Dissolve one package of dry yeast and one teaspoon of sugar in a cup of warm water. Mix with the beer liquid. Add four teaspoons salt, four tablespoons of shortening, four cups of whole rye flour and about eight cups of white flour. Proceed as with the straight dough method.

Grandma once made Beer Bread out of a heady, delinquent brew. After repeatedly punching down the bread, she put the dough into pans and into the oven where it rebelled completely. The uprising tried to climb through the grate and out the door; it demanded its "rights" to be free to do as it wished. With beery breath the dough declared that it was being discriminated against, that society (Grandma) was to blame for its erratic behavior. Grandma handled the rebellion by chucking the whole batch in the chicken yard. Yeast was good for her old hens' gizzards, she said.

Everyone knows that I love to bake bread, that I'll do anything to get my hands in dough, even someone else's dough, and one evening an electronics engineer from across the street called excitedly, "Come over, we have something to show you." Racing to their house, I bounced through the door expecting a grand surprise. "Look," whispered my host in reverent, hushed tones, as he led me into the kitchen, "Italian Bread."

They were beauties.

"I figured that if the Italians could do it, I could," my neighbor explained. "I thought about it coming home from the office; many early-day Italian-Americans were not rich, so there couldn't be much in it." He told me that he activated a package of dry yeast in a large bowl by dissolving it in one-half cup of warm water, then added one more cup of water, one tablespoon of sugar, one-and-one-half teaspoons of salt and a tablespoon of soft shortening. He mixed it well and added about four cups of flour.

After a thorough mixing he set the dough to rise for ten minutes in a warm place, cut through the dough with a spoon and repeated the ten-minute wait and cut-down by the spoon four more times.

He turned the dough onto a floured board, kneaded it gently to form two loaves, placed them on a greased baking sheet, scored the top with diagonal cuts, then covered them with a towel and let the loaves rise in a warm spot for one-and-one-half hours.

My neighbor baked his Italian Bread for thirty-five minutes at 400° F., brushed the loaves with melted butter when he took them from the oven, and watched his family of four boys devour his bread with gusto.

His future is secure. If he can't make it with his electronic stethoscope on the moon, he can make Italian Bread.

Someone once said that "hope is a poor man's bread; sweet charity is his butter." It is true that butter covers a multitude of sins; good butter soothes tempers or covers ill-raised, poorly baked bread. Good butter brings out the good, my grandmother used to tell me as I developed my skinny arm muscles turning the churn crank.

We had a glass churn which was half-filled with top cream,

and as I turned the handle, I remember wistfully watching for the butter to "come." The dasher would toss the thick liquid over and over, endlessly slopping and dashing it against the glass sides; suddenly yellow globs would catch on the wooden paddles, fat would begin to float in bunches, and abruptly golden butter held tight to the wood. It seemed as if the mass did not want to be beaten any more, and so the butter tightened itself in an effort to stop the paddles. When we unscrewed the lid and withdrew the dasher, a cheesy-like, baby-sweet breath filled the room.

Carefully, the buttermilk was poured through a strainer and saved for biscuits, the chicken trough, or a "strange neighbor man" who drank the stuff. (Today I love buttermilk and pay dearly for the cultured skim milk product.) After straining, the lump of butter was washed in cold water and worked with a wooden spoon. The yellow fat was put on a board and pressed and turned and pressed until every drop of whey was squeezed out.

Finally Grandma inspected, salted the butter with plain salt to taste (about one-eighth teaspoon salt per cup of butter), then with great ceremony dipped two wooden spoons in hot water, then in cold, and rolled the butter with them to mix and compact it before deftly picking it up and popping it into the square wooden mold with sides that fell away at a magic touch. The tops of Grandma's molds were carved inside with symbols; the flower meant sweet cream butter and the butterfly indicated that sour cream had been used. After the butter was imprinted it was wrapped in wax paper and stored in the icebox. Both sweet and sour cream make excellent butter. Both are flavored to a degree by the cow's diet: a cow on pasture gives a yellower, more intense cream; grain-fed cows give a milder golden cream.

Today, butter is whipped by giant stainless steel churns—pasteurized, colored, cut and packaged; but my grandmother's words are still true: good butter brings out the good.

Butter may be preserved in brine (one cup of salt to one quart of water) or kept fresh in water with a 3 percent solution of borax. I have not tasted borax butter but I have eaten my weight in brined butter and it stays sweet as the day it was preserved.

In Alaska, butter brined in kegs had hidden advantages. Longshoremen used to toss the small barrels of butter over the side when unloading ships, then at midnight they would walk along the beach and "find" their butter.

Brined or boraxed, butter keeps well and usually needs no leaching before use.

Goosebutter glows with good feeling. We used to render goose fat, spread it on fresh bread, sprinkle it with salt, then sink our teeth in its good nature.

I boarded with a farm family when I taught rural school in Missouri, and they had a gander called Toadstool that hissed me out of the yard and ran me up the road each day. Mrs. Halman made a savory goose butter out of old Toadstool's fat by rendering it together with two apples, two onions and a teaspoon of marjoram tied in a cloth. Strained, cooled and spread on bread, Toadstool's butter drenched every taste bud with delight. I even forgave the old gander for the ignoble manner in which he raced me to the mailbox. Plain, or seasoned, goose butter is a neglected spread, a real disadvantaged food in today's world.

Another butter we used to make at home was peanut butter, but we considered the commercial product far superior to the chunky, lumpy, oily on the top, stiff on the bottom, often rancid homemade peanut butter.

We used to roast peanuts briefly in their shells on flat tins in a low oven, then we shelled, skinned and lightly salted them. Using the finest chopper plate, we put a handful of peanuts in and ground away. The nuts would pop out all over the kitchen floor as we turned. We had a cat that chased and ate the peanuts as they scattered. A real "fat cat," she would fill up on peanuts, then saunter to the chicken yard to drink water. She'd emerge from the pen looking like a satisfied fur-coated customer emerging from a good restaurant.

After the peanuts were ground once, we mixed in one-half cup of vegetable oil and two tablespoons of sugar to the quart of peanut butter, and ground it again. The second grinding was a toil. Gluey peanut butter stuck to everything.

As a trick, if the cat had not been around when the peanuts were popping on the first grinding, Granddaddy would ask her to sit up and he'd pop a wad of peanut butter into her eager mouth. Tail snapping, eyes blazing, she'd whip around the kitchen with a grin on her face as she tried to lick it from the roof of her mouth. But she'd always come back for more, and watching her mixed-up reflexes would make the second icky grinding job go faster.

Homemade peanut butter should be made in small quantities, a quart or two at a time. The jars should be packed tightly to within one-half inch from the top and a layer of oil (soybean or salad) or clarified butter poured across the top of each jar as a seal. The jars should be lidded and refrigerated.

Homemade peanut butter separates readily and should be well mixed before using. The first several sandwiches out of the jar are the best. Lower down in the jar, the peanut butter becomes drier and stronger, but is good in peanut butter cookies, candy or soup.

When I was teaching in Missouri and used to come home "hungry as a woodchuck," Mrs. Halman would sometimes fix me a bowl of peanut butter soup. I have fixed it for our teen-aged woodchucks and they loved it. Make a paste of three tablespoons of flour and a little milk and add it, together with one-half cup of peanut butter, to a quart of milk in a double boiler. Sprinkle a small bay leaf, one-half teaspoon of celery salt and one-half teaspoon of onion salt on top, mix with a fork for about five or ten minutes. When thick, but not boiling, serve with saltine crackers.

I have not made butter with hickory nuts or walnuts. I knew a man who ground butternut meats to spread on celery sticks and crisp Jerusalem artichoke root sticks as a nature-food party treat. To extract the nut meats, he boiled the butternuts for twenty minutes, then drain and let them cool before cracking. He picked the meat and ground it into paste before adding a few drops of icy water to coagulate the oil. He did not salt or flavor his spread, and it was uniquely different. To me it had the nutty rich flavor of fresh white whale blubber. With the first mouthful I was transported in time to a frigid beach on Shelikof Strait where we landed to see if the Alaskan natives gathered there needed help. It turned out that they had killed a whale. In the icy wind small boats crowded the shore, and men were hacking out chunks of meat from the monstrous carcass. Youngsters and women stood, backs to the gale, gnawing pieces of half-frozen blubber. I joined them and was surprised by the sweet, non-fishy, nut flavor of the meat. Our suburban host's butternut butter reminded me of that elegant fare.

Soybean flour may be made into a peanutty butter. Carefully roast the soybean flour in a shallow pan in a low oven until brown. Salt lightly, mix with soybean oil and a little boiling water. Store overnight in a covered jar, and refrigerate for longer keeping. Soy butter made from roasted flour, then blended half and half with real peanut butter, is remarkably similar to commercial peanut butter in texture and taste. I have been partial to soybean products since my Depression school-days in Missouri. I used to work at odd jobs, and one of them was in an egg and feed store. That summer I lived on eggs and soybean meal.

Contemporary man nibbles nuts to assuage between-meal heebie-jeebies or to make bad beer taste better; but more primitive peoples view nut meats as a staple. American Indians of all tribes used to eat every known variety of nut. Some Indians, sneakier than others, let the squirrels do the gathering. The tribesmen gathered the nuts from the squirrels' caches, and their squaws shelled and preserved the meats before the "nut worms" gathered.

The names *Juglans* and *Hicoria* sound like characters out of a Roman drama. "Jovis glans, the acorn of Jove," was so esteemed by Europeans that in certain countries, the law required young men to plant walnut trees before they were allowed to marry. In the broadest view that would seem to be a good law for the world. Different species of walnut trees grow across nearly all sections of our earth. The planting of a tree could be construed as a tax men pay to the earth. Trees hold in moisture and give nutrients to the soil, they block out harmful rays of the sun, control erosion, manufacture gases and produce crops that man and wildlife can use. Trees belong to the earth, and by planting a tree man can support the future of the earth.

In the deep loam of river valleys from Canada to Delaware and westward into Arkansas, the hardy white walnut or butter-nut (*Juglans cinerea*) grows native and is cultivated for shade and fruit. It is a cheerful tree although vulnerable to breaking in high winds.

Butternut oil was extracted by Indians (and later by the settlers) and used as a butter or a lubricant for dried or fatless meat. The Indians husked the nuts, beat them into an oily, shell-ridden mass, then dumped them into boiling water. As the nut mixture boiled, the meats gradually separated and floated just below the topmost layer of surface oil. The butternut oil was skimmed, ladled into bark or stone containers and stored for winter "butter." Tightly lidded nut oil does not become rancid; exposed to the air it grows strong. Homemade nut oil is thick, bland and, with a sprinkle of salt, pronounced very good.

Butternut meats strained from the boiling liquid were pressed into pemmican-like cakes, salted, dried on stones near the fire and stored with straw in bladder sacks for emergency food for hunters.

The emulsion or liquid in which the nuts had been boiled was used as soup base and often added to the venison stock for a warming autumn food. Indian infants were fed butternut-venison broth as a weaning expedient. Not all the skimmed butternut broth became soup. Some tribes fermented the nut juice and drank it as a heady "nut milk."

The black walnut (*Juglans nigra*), which grows from Ontario to Florida and westward, is a majestic tree that has been abused by lumber-hungry hordes. Our family enjoys the hard-shelled black walnuts in breads, candies, cookies and in toppings. When October woods have lost their glow and browns take over the landscape, we usually strike out for the hill where a lonely walnut tree etches its blunt-ended limbs against the clouds. Black spongy spheres cling to the leafless branches, and one has only to crush a twig bud to smell the musty juice and revive all the memories of earlier nutting parties and tasty goodies. Martin usually climbs and shakes while the rest of us search the grasses and duck the falling fruit.

Some people hull nuts on the spot; we dry our walnuts under screen frames to protect them from thieving suburban squirrels, then lay them in a depression in the driveway and run the car over them. We sometimes soak the hulls in water and save the rich brown stain for wood coloring.

Picking nut meats for sale is a source of income for some rural families. One community we visited gathers a miniature mountain of walnuts each fall, then like an old-time cottage industry, families get together to "jug nuts." That is, they visit with their neighbors and pick out walnut kernels to fill earthen storage jugs. Some families eat the nut meats that have been sealed in the jugs with cork and paraffin, others sell their walnut meats. "A jug of nuts is as good as cash," one mountain mother told me.

Although walnut meats are usually mixed into cakes or

candies, everyone ate Sweet Potato and Walnut Croquettes at hog killing time in northwest Missouri. Puffy, sweet, with a musky walnut bite, these All-American croquettes complement an early winter supper of neckbones and sauerkraut. Boil and mass enough sweet potatoes to make two cups, add one cup of moderately fine-chopped nuts, beat in two tablespoons of butter, four teaspoons of cream, two eggs and a sprinkle of salt. When cool, form into croquettes, roll in egg and cracker crumbs and set in a cool place for an hour before frying in deep, boiling fat.

If you favor a meat meal without meat, Walnut Roast, a Depression-time dish, is a natural. To one-and-one-half cups of toasted bread crumbs add two cups of milk and let them soak while you beat two eggs. Fold the eggs into the crumbs and mix in one teaspoon of salt, two teaspoons of grated onions and a cup of finely chopped walnuts. Pour into a buttered baking dish and bake at 350° F. With late wild greens, early baby turnips, corn cakes and apple pie, Walnut Roast is delicious.

Sugared walnuts will keep fresh for several months (if you can hide them from your sweetmeat stealers). Make a syrup of one cup of white sugar and one cup of water. Boil until thick, or until a spoon dipped into the mixture and withdrawn is followed by a long thread. Dipped in cold water the syrup thread will become brittle. The fire must be carefully controlled at this stage or the syrup will become dark and bitter. When the syrup threads readily, drop in one-and-one-half cups of the largest nut meats, add a few drops of vanilla, stir rapidly and remove from fire. Quickly spoon the sugared nuts onto wax paper, separate, cool and serve, or store in glass jars.

For little-girl candy that is simple, safe and tasty, beat one egg white very stiff and gradually whip in confectioner's sugar to make it even stiffer. As the mixture dries, a fork will have to be substituted for the beater. Slowly add evaporated milk alternately with vanilla, a few drops at a time, and mix until the fondant becomes as thick as "Play Dough." Knead with hands and roll into balls the size of a nickel. Flatten by pressing a walnut meat into each ball. Eat.

Black walnuts are best if they are allowed to cure a few weeks before cracking. Unshelled, they need no special treatment except a varmint-proof storage area for long keeping.

One night when I was a child and alone in the house I heard

"thump, thump" repeated thirteen times, then silence. Again and again I heard thirteen hollow thumps, then quietness. A fan of the Bobbsey Twins, I was petrified at the prospect of a peg-legged intruder walking up and down the cellar stairs. I became so scared I wet the bed. As I lay in my puddle unable to move, I heard the door open and promptly fainted.

I awoke with Grandma pressing cold cloths to my head. Before I could explain what happened, Grandma squeezed me and, calling me her "juiciest angel," told me that they had returned, heard a thumping noise and found a pack rat dropping walnuts down the stairs to the basement. At that moment Grandfather stomped into my room. His large nose quivering with humor, he said, "Do you know that since we left for the lodge meeting two hours ago, that pack rat moved over a bushel of nuts? He wasn't only a greedy rat, he was a holy one, too. I found this in his nest." He held up Grandma's rosary.

Varmints: squirrels, mice and rats can steal your nuts faster than you can pick them up; they are all expert thieves.

The hickory tree (*Hicoria*) is now an American, though records have been found in tertiarian rocks indicating that the hickory was formerly a globetrotter. Today the hickory thrives from Ontario to Florida and west to Texas.

Hickory nuts may be processed, preserved and eaten like walnuts.

My young people usually call for Spiced Nuts when they have picked a pint of nut meats, so I light the oven and set it to heat at 300° F. while I mix the spices.

For Spiced Nuts: beat one egg white and slowly stir in one tablespoon of melted butter and two cups of nuts. In a second bowl mix one cup of sugar, one-half teaspoon of salt, one-and-a-half teaspoons of cinnamon and three-fourths teaspoon each of nutmeg and allspice.

Spread one-fourth of the sugar-spice on a cookie sheet, coat the nuts a few at a time in the rest of the sugar-spice mixture and lay them on the cookie tin. Sprinkle any sugar-spice remaining in the bowl over the nuts.

Pop the tin into the oven and bake about fifteen minutes, or until the nuts are pale brown.

Remove the cookie sheet, stir the spiced nuts gently to separate them and pour them onto wax paper to cool. If there are any left, store in a glass jar.

Chopped hickories in sour cream with a little grated onion, salt and pepper make an interesting and nutritious topping for baked potatoes, or asparagus.

My grandmother used to can rhubarb sauce with nuts in it, and Granddaddy loved it heaped on pork chops.

Hickory Stuffing for roasted chicken is very good.

Grandma had a striped hen given to her by the mailman as a thank-you for the cookies and tea she had out for him on hot days. Grandma was very proud of her Barred Rock because the postman said it had come from champion stock. (The hen's father had been named "Cockerel of the Year" by a regional poultry fraternity.) Granddaddy took one look at the fat black-and-white hen, said she was not laying and declared she would make a fine Sunday dinner. Besides, he added, the hen thought she was a rooster and tried to boss the chicken yard.

Their squabble went on for over a year. Then one evening Granddaddy arrived at the kitchen door holding a headless, plucked and drawn hen.

That was a good fight. But things quieted after a while and we ate Barred Rock the following day. As we munched on that delicious golden hen and crunched on Hickory Stuffing, Granddaddy told of the chicken's last act. "She got me right here," he said, rolling up his pants leg to show a tremendous bruise where the hen had flown up and spurred him. "When I went after her, she flew into the garage and took cover in the car engine. I had the hood up. She made an awful noise. Suddenly there were feathers everywhere and she lost her cackle." It seems that Granddaddy had the engine running and the hen had stuck her head in the fan.

For quite a few weeks after that, whenever Granddaddy started the Essex feathers would fly and Grandma would get mad all over again.

Hickory Stuffing is simplicity itself. Make a stuffing with broken bread seasoned with eggs, butter, pepper and salt, then mix in a cup of chopped hickory nuts. Stuff and roast your hen, or bake hickory dressing with pork chops.

Once I tried to make catsup from hickory nuts. I got as far as putting salt between layers of half-grown nuts, looked into the crock and saw little green worms squiggling out of the soft nuts. I didn't study the situation. I threw out my hopes for tangy hickory catsup. Grandma would have taken the nuts to the chicken yard. When she had extra nuts she would have me crack a bunch and throw them to the chickens. Chicks and hogs love nuts, she said.

A bachelor neighbor in the country fries hickories or English walnuts. Salted, they contain all the pleasures of a frisky autumn night. Briefly, fry two cups of the biggest pieces of nuts in one cup of hot olive or cooking oil. Do not allow to remain in the oil too long. Drain on paper, sprinkle with salt, pour yourself a beer and sit back to munch; all the tingly, crunchy, warm, rich goodness of the earth's trees gather happily around your tonsils.

One Saturday I had aspirations of perpetuating fine fat hickory nut trees and planted twenty-five nuts in a hand-dug trench. With slyness I scattered leaves to camouflage my handiwork. The following Saturday I returned to find that the Culpeper County squirrels had dug out every nut and absconded with my prize specimens. I have found that squirrels will even eat the nut bases of six-inch seedling trees, and that they are not discouraged by wire, traps or gunshots. A good dog seems to be one answer if you wish to raise your very own nut trees in squirrel country, or, my neighbor advised, plant a nut and place over it a tin can (top removed and the inverted can bottom cut open to form a cross). Next year I am going to plant a few nuts with tin-can foils and see if I can outsmart the squirrels.

There was a belief in olden days throughout Europe that if you wished to leave an inheritance you planted a tree. Today, inheritance often tends to mean material goods. Yet time and again world forces destroy that which man creates. Sons are left with legacies that have lost their place and function in society.

As long as there is an earth, trees will give a true inheritance. Nut trees give more than most trees. In addition to beauty, shade, moisture, mulch, lumber, fuel, acids, oils and oxygen, their fruit is food. Nut trees are one of the most elegant gifts we can leave for our unborn generations.

Shells of hickory and walnuts have natural preserving qualities, but other fruits are not so well endowed. Living the natural life demands preserving; and as the mod bra ad reads, "When nature does not provide, man should improvise."

I became interested in preserving our own fruit by drying during the "year of the peach." After canning, freezing, pickling, preserving, brandying and brewing in every container available, I turned to dehydration. I found drying fruit to be simple and the product a popular treat in school lunches and afternoon snacks. Since experimenting with peaches I have dried apples, pears, grapes and plums; they all keep well and, with the exception of grapes, they are delicious.

Sun-drying of surplus is the most primitive and the least expensive method of saving food.

Records show that squash and pumpkins were among the fruits most commonly dried by American Indians and colonial peoples of the north temperate zones. The seedless strips of squash were threaded on fibers and hung on trees or racks to dry. Later they were brought into the home and hung above the fireplace or stove.

I have not dried winter squash but I have dried pumpkin. One caution: do not allow the drying slices to become wet by rain or they will melt. My pumpkin rings, hanging lustrous and orange on the clothesline, turned black after being left out in the rain and they literally dripped into long dark stalactites, oozed down to the lawn and disappeared.

Each year I dry the fullest, mature squash and pumpkin seeds for nibbles. I clean most of the fleshy strings from the seeds, lay them on a paper towel, turn them two or three times a day for about a week, and when they are fully dry, I store them in a coffee tin. When we need a quick bit of energy, the seeds are briefly fried (two or three minutes) in salad oil, drained on paper, salted and eaten. These oil-roasted squash seeds do not keep and must be eaten within the hour. They appear to absorb moisture and soon become tough and tasteless as straw. Fresh-roasted dried seeds are as irresistible as buttery popcorn.

Sunflower seeds are another challenge to the choppers. Most years we drop in a garden row of sunflowers to feed the birds, snatch a few for nibbles and to observe the wondrous heliotropism (turning to face the sun) manifested by the plant. We have found that it is best to plant the heavy-headed varieties such as Mammoth Russian or Jumbo sunflower seed, because if the flowers hold their heads upright your feathered friends sit on top and eat all of your profits. Birds have a bit more trouble hanging on when the flower is upside down.

Indians used sunflower seeds for food, oil and soap. They made bread by parching and pounding the seeds, then mixing them with marrow before baking them in cakes on hot stones.

My grandfather planted sunflower seeds in four-inch-deep holes into which he had put some chicken droppings. His stalks grew ten feet tall. He planted in May and harvested in October when "the birds began to show interest." I harvest sunflower seed heads about the last of September by cutting the head with a foot of stalk attached; the center seeds are not mature, but it's a tossup: wait until the center has matured and the birds have pecked out the full seed rings, or cut sunflowers with filled outer seeds and chaff in the middle.

In either case, the seed heads should be hung in a dry, airy place to cure for about a month before they are picked out, dried for a few more days and stored.

Boys, mice, little squirrels and girls love to scavenge sunflower seeds. A friend said that she had saved me some Sungold seed. (I am a seed moocher of the worst kind. Actually I remember people by their seeds. It's a pleasant bad habit.) We went to the shed and examined dozens of downward-hanging Sungold heads—not one seed. The lady's grandson stood grinning guiltily in the doorway.

Sunflower seeds may be eaten raw or briefly roasted in hot oil or in the oven. My grandfather roasted his nibbles in the oven, about 300° F., for approximately ten minutes, then salted and ate them. You have to have a talented tongue and cooperative teeth to attack sunflower seeds successfully. I have never really mastered the technique. I usually let the seed swim around till I catch it, chomp it into bits and spit out pieces of shell. An expert sunflower-seed eater does not crack the shell—he somehow pries it open and evicts the kernel.

Preserving fruit by drying in the sun still prevails in some parts of the country. In the South I have seen rows of boards tilted up to the sun and covered with sliced fruit. Sometimes the sliced fruit is spread between sheets of muslin, which keeps away insects and gives the fruit a better color. New Englanders pared, quartered and strung apples on string with a needle, then hung them on the sunny side of the house when I was a child, and I suspect the practice is still observed in some areas. My grandmother used to string apples and pears and hang them in the attic after a three-day hot-sun treatment.

The basic equipment needed for early-day sun-drying fruit was a needle and light string, or nonmetal racks.

One extra step, the sulphuring of fruit to be dried, is added today. Equipment and supplies for sulphuring fruit are: powdered sulphur (obtainable at drug stores), small pieces of paper in which to wrap the sulphur for burning, a tin or dish to hold the smoldering sulphur, a large box that will fit over the racks of fruit and the sulphur dish, and clean cheesecloth.

Try to dry fruit on bright, hot days when the air is moving. Air should circulate around food to dry it as quickly as possible. Cleanliness is a prime rule, and because bruised fruit readily ferments, all produce should be checked carefully for defects. Bacteria, like bored children, have a tendency to hang around looking for something to get into; so fruit should be dried as fast as possible, in clean surroundings, and it should have no bruises.

To dry or dehydrate fruit to preserve it, pick firm, ripe fruit at the eating stage, then carefully wash it in cold water. Peel, core or slice if desired, then sulphur the fruit. Though not essential, sulphur retards spoilage, helps to retain vitamins and adds rich color to fruit.

Lay the fresh fruit one layer deep on nonmetal trays that are slotted or perforated to allow the circulation of air. Stack the trays, separating them about one-and-one-half inches from each other with blocks of wood. Place the lowest tray on bricks so that it will be raised four inches off the ground. Sulphur fumes must circulate around all of the fruit.

Allow one tablespoon of dry sulphur for each pound of prepared fruit. Wrap the sulphur in a small piece of paper, roll and loosely twist the ends so that the paper can be lighted. Place the paper containing the sulphur in the shallow tin (such as a frozen food plate) and set the tin by the side of the stacked trays of fruit. Light the paper and quickly cover the stack of trays and the smoldering sulphur with a large wood or cardboard box. The box should be fairly tight to prevent loss of fumes.

Most peeled and sliced large fruits—apples, pears and peaches, as well as pitted and halved plums and apricots— should be treated with sulphur fumes for one hour.

After sulphuring, spread the fruit evenly one layer deep on clean trays, cover the fruit loosely with cheesecloth (fastened so that it will not blow off) and place the trays in the sun.

Direct sunlight is best for drying fruit, so one edge of the drying trays may have to be elevated with a block. Elevating the trays also permits air to circulate under the fruit.

Trays of sun-drying fruit should be laid in an area away from people, dust, dirt and animals. They should be off the ground to avoid dampness, and taken inside when there is a chance of rain. My grandmother brought her drying fruit inside at night so that they would not "sweat."

Fruit should be turned two or three times a day.

When two-thirds dry, or if when squeezed the fruit leaves no moisture on your hand, take the fruit from the trays, pack loosely in a large container, and cover with a cloth. Leave the fruit to cure in the house for eight to ten days, stirring two or three times each day.

Pack the dried fruit in small moisture-, insect- and dirt-proof containers with tight lids, and store in a clean, cool, dark, dry place.

I have sun-dried fruit without the sulphur treatment by laying the prepared fruit slices on nonmetal screens in the sun and turning them often. I take the fruit into the house at night. When the initial water has evaporated, I spread the fruit one deep on wax paper on the kitchen counter to cure for a week or ten days. Of course we nibble, but I usually manage to save some of the fruit from nimble fingers and preserve it in vacuum-packed jars.

To vacuum-pack I wash, sterilize and dry pint jars and the lids. I pack them with the dried fruit, lid them tightly, then put the jars in the oven and turn on the heat to the lowest possible degree. Gradually, over a period of several hours, I elevate the heat to 225° F., then turn it off. I let the jars cool overnight in the oven. At no time after I put the glass jars into the oven do I open the door until the next morning when the bottles are cool and sealed. I am a coward around flying glass. The dried fruits are tasty, moist and sweet.

Oven-dried fruits are often less sweet because the starches are not converted to sugars; however, in some areas ovens are the only practical way to dry fruit. Oven drying should start at a temperature of about 150° F.; then the heat is gradually reduced to 100° F. The prepared fruit should be layered one deep on enamel-coated racks in the oven. A pan of water on the oven floor will provide moist heat. Moisture insures that the fruit will dry from the inside out as it does in an airy, sunny situation.

A neighbor who oven-dries apples props the door partly open and gives the fruit short treatments with the heat on and then off. He cures his oven-dried fruit in his garage for a week "so the cat hair won't get in it." (They have long-haired cats and the fur flies around their house.) After his fruit is cured he stores it in jars with tight lids and he and his wife enjoy the apples as midwinter nibbles.

Drying fruit, though an ancient art, may also be considered mod because of its utility and earthly simplicity. The product meets modern standards, too: attractive, easy to prepare, tasty and natural. Dried peaches, pears and apples are busy-life food —snatch and pop, sweet dehydration!

Candy is usually thought of as tidbit food, but it was also one of the earliest methods of preserving the produce of our homeland. Many fruits, nuts and roots were crystallized as a means of saving them. Pansies, violets, roses and mint were candied into flowery sweets. Ginger and sassafras, sweetflag and elecampane roots were candied into stronger confections. Native nuts, chestnuts, peanuts, cocoanuts, citrus peelings, figs, cherries, plums and strawberries—all have been glacéd into sweet dainties by early Americans.

To make candy, a heavy pot and a long-handled spoon are the basic needs. Sugar is the basic ingredient, and management of the heat is the primary skill involved in candy making.

When I was a child I used to visit my Grand-aunt Josephine, who lived in an ornate house with a magnificent turret-top porch, a leggy apricot tree that hung over the outside stairs to the tower porch, and dwarf cherry trees in the back garden. I cannot remember the appearance of my Aunt Josephine but I remember her spy-high retreat where she dried apricots and candy cherries in the sun. I used to sit surrounded by the percolating fruit and listen to the town noises below.

To candy cherries (and later each summer, apricots) Aunt Josephine washed and pitted her fruit, then layered it in a bowl with sugar, using two-and-one-half cups of sugar for each five cups of prepared fruit. The mixture was allowed to stand overnight and the next morning she simmered the fruit for about twenty minutes. She removed the sugared cherries from the stove, let them stand a second night and again simmered them for twenty minutes. If the syrup was not absorbed by the fruit she repeated the process the following day. When the cherries were nearly void of juice she carried them to the turret top and spooned each glassy piece of fruit onto trays of wax paper. She allowed them to dry in the sun, and when all moisture was sealed, she stored the tart, bright spheres in sterilized, dry containers. When Aunt Josephine came to visit on Holy Days I'd peep into her satchel to see if she remembered. Her gifts of candied fruit mingle in my memory with visions of her lovable, mixed-up house.

Candied peach (pear or plum) paste is a simple, tasty confection. Cut the ripe fruit into small pieces and put them into a large, heavy pan with a wee bit of water. Reduce by boiling, stirring constantly, until thick and plopping. Remove from fire. For each pound of pulp make a syrup of one pound of sugar which has been previously mixed and boiled with one-half cup of water until a soft-ball stage is reached. (When a tiny bit of the boiling sugar syrup, dropped in cold water, forms a soft ball.) Mix the hot fruit plup with the hot soft-ball-stage syrup and return the mixture to the fire for a short time. Stir constantly. When the paste has nearly boiled dry, pour it on an oiled surface and spread as thin as desired. Break apart when cool. Peach paste may be packed between layers of waxed paper and stored in tightly lidded cans.

Glacé cherries, figs, plums or pears are more fruit sweets. Wash, dry and stone any firm fruit and cover with a boiling syrup made half and half, sugar and water. Boil for ten minutes, cool overnight. Repeat for four days. Remove from the fire after the final boiling, drain the fruit into a colander, shake off moisture and place the fruit on trays in an oven, pre-heated to 200° F. Turn off the heat and shut the door. Let the fruit remain in the over overnight or until they are dry or glacéd. These fruits will not keep well unless vacuum-sealed in jars. Opened jars should be stored in the icebox and checked for signs of fermentation before use. I have used slightly fermented fruits on ice cream and it was great. A neighbor in Florida said she used to feed the winey sweet fruit to her daughter to quiet her when she was teething. She said, "It sure stops the yammering."

Nut meats preserved in sugar are called brittles. I had an Alaskan friend who made nut brittle by the lard-tin full.

For a small batch of nut brittle, put three pounds of sugar into a heavy pan and heat over a fire, stirring constantly until the sugar dissolves into a brown liquid.

Remove from the fire and stir in two pounds of unsalted Spanish peanuts, or native nuts. Place again on the fire and stir until the nuts are well covered and heated through. Add a pinch of salt and one teaspoon of soda. The brittle will foam. Stir fast and pour at once onto an oiled slab of marble. As the brittle cools, work and stretch it with your hands until thin. Allow the brittle to remain on the marble until cold, then break it and pack in a cool, dry place.

Although marble is a superior surface, I have used a well-greased cookie tin for nut brittle; the candy cools a little fast for the best possible stretching, but we eat and enjoy it anyway.

Honey fudge is an early American confection which I learned about in Missouri and which we made with hickory and black walnuts. Scald one-quarter cup of milk, lower the fire and mix in one-and-one-half cups of honey with some comb included. When melted and well blended, add one-and-one-half cups of chopped and pitted dates and one-and-one-half cups of chopped nuts and a pinch of salt. Boil gently, stirring constantly until a firm, soft ball forms when a bit of the liquid is dropped into cold water. Remove from the heat and, when tepid, beat until the fudge becomes light-colored and stiff. Spread on a greased shallow platter, and cut into squares.

Honey fudge was always a treat in our house because we had dates only at Christmas time. We planned the use of each individual date, and mercy on anyone caught snitching some.

Grandma hid her Christmas goodies in some unique places: the hall closet, where she kept boxes of her good shoes, was a favorite. If you had a discerning nose you could tell which were shoes without getting the boxes down. Under the seat of the hat rack in the front vestibule was another sneaky place in which she hid holiday treats. The whole entryway smelled anisey. Her customary spot to keep honey fudge was under Granddaddy's handkerchiefs in his sock drawer. I remember filching three or four pieces one time when I was supposed to be asleep in bed. I fell asleep, all right, but not before I had hidden some of my stolen candy in the breast pocket of my pajamas. When I awoke the next morning, the bedsheet, my pajama top and my hair were a gooey mess; I was caught. Stolen fruits may seem sweetest to some robbers, but this thief got stuck.

I have read that honey is a natural preservative, that meat, vegetables, fruits and nuts were stored in crocks of honey and sealed with beeswax during colonial times. I have always wanted to locate a honey tree (to try my hand at sweet saving), but the one tree Lewis and I stalked out believing it to be a happy hive of honeys turned out to harbor evil-tempered hornets.

My grandfather studied bees, and although we did not keep them, he scouted wild bee trees in early spring by tracking "bee-lines" from fields of "blue blooms" to the comb. He believed that blue flowers contained a substance that honey bees craved at the end of the winter, and on bright mornings in April or May he would take his fishing pole and head for the flatlands where hyacinths, violets, cowslips and bluets nodded with busy bee visitors. It is best to bee-watch in the morning, after the sun has warmed the air but before ground insects confuse the buzzing scene. My grandfather said he could distinguish the hum of a nectar-heavy honey, but to my untrained ear, a hum is a hum. Also, with today's sound-saturated atmosphere, simply hearing a hum is a feat.

As the worker bees foraged flower dust and flitted home, Granddaddy stood listening, waiting and watching for straight-line flights along honey bee airlanes. Sometimes it took him four days (actually only a few hours a day, because he always liked to wet a line), and sometimes he studied bee flights for weeks before he discovered a hideaway in the near-leafless woods. As he approached a bee tree, my grandfather told of the sense of vibration he felt in his "pores." He usually marked the honey tree, and just before fall he rounded up a raiding party and everyone carried buckets as they tramped after honey.

If possible, the bee men tried to subdue the hive by a sudden thwacking on the tree trunk or by shooting a gun a little before dawn on the gray, usually wet morning they chose to go after honey. Abrupt, loud reports are said to cause the bees to rally around the queen and form a ball.

Once I tried to corral a swarm by cracking two boards together. The insects dived for our porch and alighted on the screen door. By the time everyone finished running in and out, the bees had scattered.

Bee trees are supposedly easy to locate in midsummer when the old queens drive the upstart would-bees from the nest, or when the old gals stomp off to sulk in a new pad. Emigrating bees are often lethargic because they stuff themselves with honey before they leave home. With their stomachs full they fly a ways and have to stop for a siesta before swarming again.

If you follow an emigrating swarm, mark the site, and your calendar, as a reminder to rob the hive the following year. Don't steal from a new hive. A year's effort goes into building and storing enough honey to sustain a queen bee's entourage.

If you are a bee-watcher in the fall, look low. Be on the watch for crumpled or discarded pieces of beehive wax at the base of a big, often partly rotted tree. Torn comb on the ground indicates that a bear or other thief beat you to the honey. Mark the tree, then eleven months later beat your furry competitor to the sweet. Animals raid but are usually driven off before they destroy the hive.

On unseasonably warm, sunny days in winter, honey bees often buzz down to the corner for a short beer. Buzzing is easily discernible in the stillness of the snowy woods, and honey trees may be marked for a little latter-day thievery.

It is important to study the whole layout of a wild bee tree, a barn or walled enclosure before stealing honey. Try not to destroy the hive, but if destruction is inevitable, wait until spring for your honey. Bees cannot survive the winter without food and protection.

My grandfather told me that there are chemicals to subdue bees but that his bee-raiding parties used a smudge to smoke the bees into a hysteria that prompted them to gorge honey and go to sleep. He said that when the honey bees are under sedation from overeating, a man can, with slow, deliberate movement, work among them without being stung.

The one time I went with my grandfather to gather honey, the men cut a leaning tree after listening with their ears cupped against it. I was told that the area below the noisiest part of the hollow trunk was thought to contain old honey. Apparently that which our party stole was old; it smelled and looked like soured moose milk. My grandfather sometimes brought home buckets of scrambled comb, honey and bees that had to be melted and separated, but often he brought perfect chunks of heavy, dark comb honey.

Although my grandfather found dozens of bee trees in northwest Missouri and always was glad to get honey, I never saw him raid a tree or handle the insects. I think he was afraid of bees.

During the war I worked for a medical doctor who kept bees and who held great faith in honey. He reserved on his desk a jar of orange-blossom nectar (from his own hives) into which he often mixed an equal quantity of finely chopped nuts. As some of his patients talked to him, he'd spoon out a paper cup of the sticky sweet and hand it to the person together with a wooden tongue depressor. He'd tell them to eat it. Although Doctor prescribed modern drugs and often referred his patients to specialists, he believed that natural sweetening in the diet, honey, was compatible with good health. He believed that natural talk-it-out sessions were valuable. He often used honey and nuts as a springboard for discussions.

"Just think," he would sometimes explode from his desk beside his startled patient. "Beeswax, like love, holds sweetness and life. It protects, confines, it is supple and giving."

"Honey is an outward sign of faith. Faith because honey is a natural example of saving for the future," the doctor would tell his patients.

"Nuts are the seed of tomorrow. Without seed there would be no trees; no gases to protect the land from the harmful rays of the sun."

His patients would gape in wonderment, then gobble up his nut honey and his words.

"For a happy, healthy life, there must be a tomorrow," the doctor would declare. And all who heard believed him.

11

Safekeeping

Living the natural life, preserving a life in harmony with all things entails a pledge to safeguard the earth for the unborn generations of all things. Living the natural life implies safekeeping.

Preserving the earth's gifts of meat, herbs and fruit is one tiny contribution toward saving our overburdened and lacerated planet. In turn, the very act of saving becomes an act of faith because when a person saves he is saying that there will be a tomorrow. A faith in the future of our earth renews a faith in God, it supports hope and joy, as well as a concern for all people and for all things. Thus, faith becomes, as Tolstoy said, a force of life. Safekeeping that faith is a safeguard against man's destruction of his world.

Saving, whether it involves bits and pieces of meat, the gathering and brewing of native teas, or canning of the season's surplus, adds the firm touch of earthiness to today's plastic-wrapped patterns of living. Saving foods in the home cuts down on disposable refuse—garbage becomes garbage—potato peelings, stalks and bones replace foam and cardboard cartons, because in canning and curing the containers may be used over and over again. Preserving in the home rewards a family with a oneness of purpose; pickles shed their far-away-factory identity and become an extension of the family that raised them from their seedy infancy, through their pickle-puppy years to sophisticated citizens of the fermenting crock.

Conserve, preserve, pickle or brine; cure, corn, kipper or jerk; dry, smoke, can or pot; the safekeeping of food is fun.

Saving food is a challenging confrontation between the microbe world and man's ingenuity. Bacteria may be the bad guys (those that cause disease and spoilage in food) or they may wear the white hats (fermentation, nitrogen-fixing microorganisms, and bacteria that convert organic matter into soluble plant food). Most bacteria are parasites and need moisture, warmth and food to survive. Thus, if meat is deprived of water, bacteria that encourage spoilage will be inhibited. Generally speaking, bacteria are retarded by a 15 percent or stronger brine. Salt removes the body fluids from meat and partly replaces the fluids with salt solution. Salt alters tissues so that osmosis is slowed and drying takes place.

Whether meat is to be dried, pickled, corned, smoked or jerked, salt (dry or in brine) is the first requirement for safekeeping. Dry salt is usually rubbed on the larger pieces at the rate of eight to ten pounds of salt per one hundred pounds of meat. Brine is made by dissolving eight to ten pounds of salt in five gallons of water for the initial curing period. Spices, sugar, saltpeter, smoke or sunlight are flavoring and preserving additives to salt. For safeguarding salted meat, cold temperatures (38° to 48° F.) retard spoilage by bacteria. To protect cured meat from insects and dust, and to prevent excessive drying, cured meats should be wrapped in brown paper and stored in a dry, dark, clean, cool place.

Sausage making adheres to the same general rules for safekeeping larger cuts of meat, and although sausage may be ground from scraps of any kind of meat, pork fat (20 to 30 percent of the total weight) is usually added to all kinds of meat because it moistens, remains soft, and is mild-flavored. Ready-to-eat sausages containing pork should be pre-frozen at minus-10° F. for twenty-one days to preclude the danger of contracting trichinosis. Some pork sausages may be cooked and this eliminates the tricky trichinae, too.

In addition to preserving the larger pieces of meat in salt cure and the trim in sausage, some parts of the carcass are potted.

Meat to be potted should be thoroughly cooked, boned, salted, seasoned and mashed into sterilized pots, then sealed with fat and stored in a cool place. Before the days when the disadvantaged portions of a beef or pig were mashed into bolognas, potted meat was the jiffy food in most households. Potting, the age-old method of saving, offers tender, simple foods, and should not be scorned.

The identifying, gathering and drying of native tea herbs is an ever-expanding pleasure; there is a tea for every mood in the natural life.

Sweet goldenrod, Oswego, verbena, and ground ivy brew into spirited infusions for occasions when neighbors gather to enjoy conversation.

Chamomile, sweet birch, fennel, slippery elm, and linden are agreeable and soothing friends.

Labrador tea is a tough old leaf, but mellow as a gruff-voiced old father when his sons return to visit. The Indians of northern America believed that this evergreen was a great chief's son returned and they drank Labrador in homage to the life spirit.

Vervain, spice bush and Virginia snakeroot teas are known as love potion drinks.

Rose hip, parsley, persimmon leaf and nettle tea are brewed for their health-giving qualities.

Basil tea, marjoram, thyme and savory are musty refreshers to be served when knotty problems snarl the senses or after a good fight. Their robust good humor clears the brain.

Technique is all-important in making tea. Authorities generally agree that you should use one teaspoon of leaf herb per person, cover with boiling water and let the tea steep for from three to five minutes.

Root teas are gourmet specials, and most roots may be used over and over. Many people prefer root teas such as ginger, licorice, sassafras or sarsaparilla roots; they let them steep longer and cover the teacup with their saucer to hold in the spicy aroma.

There are dozens of native teas to choose from and each lends its individual personality to the cup. Some are impudent acquaintances, strong-minded and favored only in small sips; some native herbs are heavy heady brews, some are wild and repulsive until you get to know them; some teas stimulate and others are quiet like a sweet memory. The cardinal rule of gathering and brewing woodland tea is *identify*. Some teas are deadly.

"God has sent us devils to rid us of our devils," a preacher once proclaimed when his fizzy sarsaparilla blew up at a tent meeting and deluged a nearby covey of reformed alcoholics.

The safekeeping of soft beers demands strict adherence to the recipe (usually a scant teaspoon of yeast to four pounds of sugar and five gallons of water). Fizzy coolers should be canned in strong bottles, capped tightly, stored in a protected area and chilled before opening.

Timing is the cue for good brew. Although the processes for making wine, beer and soft drinks are similar, the time of sealing varies. Soft beers are sealed to stop most of the yeast action (thus restricting the production of alcohol) almost immediately after mixing. Beers are allowed to ferment and convert most of the sugar into alcohol before being sealed. Wines usually go dead, that is, the yeasts use up all of the sugar possible, before they are sealed.

All fizz drinks and bottled brews should be handled with extreme care and tasted on their own merit.

Pickling or fermenting vegetables is a unique and ancient method used to preserve and flavor food. Sauerkraut, the king of fermented vegetables, reigns with his numerous cucumber princes, but other vegetables such as string beans, green tomatoes, beets, melons, corn, cauliflower and peppers may be fermented into royal cousins. The vegetables to be pickled are submerged in a brine, kept warm, 75° to 85° F. for a week or so, or until fermentation is completed, skimmed, then maintained under a brine that prevents all bacterial action, and sealed with paraffin. Some vegetables ferment faster than others because their sugar content is higher. Spinach, Swiss chard and dandelions are members of the vegetable anti-defamation league, and like proper anti-defamers they refuse to be corrupted by kraut-type bacteria. Mixing such greenery with one-fourth their weight in dry salt will crock them for posterity.

A 5 percent brine, usually used for firming vegetables, is made by dissolving three-fourths cup of salt in one gallon of water. This permits rapid fermentation, but will not preserve foods.

A 10 percent brine, used in fermenting most vegetables, is made by dissolving one-and-one-half cups of salt in one gallon of water.

A 15 percent brine, used to store fermented vegetables, is made by dissolving two-and-one-quarter cups of salt in one gallon of water.

Salt may be removed from fermented or dry-salted vegetables by soaking them in fresh water.

I had a grand-uncle whose early-morning face looked like a freshly opened potted cheese. Wrinkled, gray, gritty, and gaunt, Uncle Fritz resembled a pot of cheese in other ways, too; his true depth and spirit did not show itself until you saw into his heart. "Heaven lies hidden in all living things," he used to say as he cut into a pot of cheese and dipped his head to smell its "hidden heaven."

Cheese is the result of living microorganisms in milk and, as in other fermented products, the stopping of the fermentation process is vital to fine cheese. Potting, the sealing of cheese in pots, by the use of salt and/or fat, stops excessive bacterial action and seals in spirit and depth.

In today's splendid supermarkets it is simple to purchase odd-ball spores (in natural cheeses) and let them infiltrate your milk. Plagiarizing commercial cheeses in your own icebox, creating your own potted pleasures with milk, is an inventive pastime for those who wish to touch base with natural happenings yet are unable to scratch the soil or bottle happiness.

The habit of satisfying self "now," the bondage to self, enslaves and confines men, yet today's baying after instant liberation and freedom to "do one's own thing," the pleas heard from the margins of society, doom the pleaders to inward-looking isolation. Men who run after the rapid satisfaction of personal desires create a glass-walled vacuum about themselves like canned vegetables or fruits. The vacuum-packed men may enjoy envy and admiration but little love or freedom permeates their self-seeking situation. Marginal people cannot hope to gain real liberation from their "canned" position until they accept the responsibility for all men and for the safekeeping of our earth. Men who seek to satisfy desires created for self are fated to remain "canned" until they themselves loosen the vacuum cap and pledge themselves to serve God, Earth or other men.

A scholarly, wiry, weasel-framed, nit-picking professor who nearly flunked me because I was two days late submitting a term paper explained "inward-looking isolation" to me, and I have tried to relate his thoughts to all manner of marginal men. I have associated it with my own life before I married, with prisoners, with the "trying teen" years and with other social situations when acceptance by the main flow of life seemed to be discouraged. While canning each summer, I remember my teacher and I sometimes mentally pop him into a bottle for my own self-satisfaction.

I love to can, though. The rules of safekeeping food by canning are simple: relax, pretend you are in a spa. It is also important to select the proper method: open-kettle method for pickles and jams, boiling-water-bath method for acid or acid-treated foods, and steam-pressure method for low-acid produce and meats. Plan ahead and on canning day examine jars and lids before sterilizing them and preparing the fruits and vegetables. Muster all the help you can beg, borrow or coerce; involvement makes the food taste better. Read the directions; the deadly *Botulium clostridium* thrives in undercooked, vacuum-packed foods. Fill the jars and process the produce according to the recipe. Cool the canned goods in a draft-free place and store when cooled, then sit back and enjoy your canned endeavors all winter.

A very poor black who nevertheless walked with great elegance told us, "Every process has its law." We were giving him a lift into town when the significance of his wilderness philosophy struck us and we questioned him. The lone man, a bachelor, had made a batch of bread that morning, and had set the dough to rise, when he remembered that it was his sister's birthday. Bundling the dough, he put it under his overcoat and was hoofing down the road when we picked him up. With a good-natured laugh he brought forth his fragrant dough and rode with it on his lap. "This lump contains the great secret of the world," he told us, patting the pale bread dough. "It's hidden. Earthly bread or call it bread of heaven; the process of the risen bread is bound by law."

I would have liked to talk with the man longer but he tucked his dough beneath his coat and swung out of the car at a stop light. Thanking us, he said he'd step over to his sister's, that she enjoyed fresh-baked bread, that she was blind, and he didn't have anything else to give her. The man's words tumbled into the car, then the door slammed and he was gone.

Baking bread in the home is gladness itself; all the senses worship: sight, smell, taste, touch, the sixth sense of love; only the sense of hearing is not involved, but if you listen to the groans of pleasuring eaters, homemade bread becomes audible.

There are two main methods of making bread: the straight dough method, in which the ingredients are mixed with yeast in the morning, and the dough is raised and baked on the same day; and the sponge method, which is usually started the night before baking day.

Strong wheat flours contain gluten, which gives elasticity to dough, and bran, bean and whole grain flours such as oat and rye contain less gluten; thus they should be mixed with wheat flour for light bread.

Fermentation of yeast and flour sugars changes sugars to carbon dioxide gas and alcohol, which in turn leavens the bread. Baking stops the fermentation action and safeguards the loaf for future use. Baking bread, as with other fermentation dealings, is an easygoing, easily varied chore and its rewards of praise and good health are easy to take. As my grandmother repeated, "Nothing is more certain than bread."

With bread comes butter and waiting for the butter to "come" when pushing the churn handle was the hardest task in early-day kitchens. Butter may be made from sweet or sour cream, salted (one-eighth of a teaspoon to a cup of butter) or it may be eaten unsalted. Butter may be preserved by submerging it in a strong brine (one cup of salt dissolved in one quart of water), and sealing the container with wax.

Nut butters (actually nut oils) were historically used as lubricants for wild meats because the fat on game animals was often strong-tasting and had to be removed. In recent days, nut butters that contain ground nut meats as well as the oils are used as spreads. Nature has provided nuts with their own safe-keeping shell, so native nuts, hickories, butternuts and walnuts need only to be hulled and allowed to mature a few weeks before being eaten. Man, however, should take care to safeguard his gathered nuts against sneaky squirrels and other expert robbers from the woodlands.

Nut trees give a rich inheritance to mankind and to the earth alike; in addition to food and lumber, oil and fuel, trees hold back erosion and shield the soil from the dehydrating rays of the sun. Nut trees grow in every part of the world, from rich crop land to barren slopes. The old European law requiring a man to plant a tree before he was allowed to marry might well be reconsidered as a measure to help safeguard the earth.

Seeds such as mature squash, pumpkin and sunflower seeds are excellent food. Either nibbled raw when dried, or eaten after a brief roasting, they are all fine-flavored and fun. The only thing you have to do to preserve pumpkin seeds is to hide them from the youngsters.

Once while on a streetcar, I remember being entranced by an elderly gentleman who devoured sunflower seeds like a machine. He was sitting across from me, and I watched him insert the seeds, point-end-up, into one corner of his mouth and remove an empty hull from the other corner with no break in motion. Fantastic! He carried his nibbles in his coat pocket, and with one hand he'd reach in for a pinch, insert the seed and remove the hull. From time to time, he'd stand when the car stopped and toss a palmful of empties out the open door. Fascinated, I watched him for twenty minutes. Suddenly I was aghast to see the man stand and accidently work his partial plate into his hand and throw it out of the car with the sunflower seed shells. There was all sorts of downtown traffic below us when he leaped after his teeth. Perhaps the biggest miracle, next to his survival without injury, was the fact that he rescued his unharmed bridge, wiped it off, put it back into his mouth, and resumed his seat and his nibbling as if no crisis had occurred. Sunflower seeds are said to contain considerable vitamin B, which may have accounted for his iron-clad nerves and sturdy constitution.

Sun-drying fruits and vegetables is an age-old method of preserving food. Drying removes water, and thus the bacteria that cause spoilage are inhibited from growing. Most every kind of food may be dried, but some fruits are easier to dry than others because of moisture-content variations. Foods most commonly dried are:

Safekeeping

Fruits	Vegetables
Apples	Beans, kidney, lima and pinto
Apricots	Beans, lentils, soy (dried in
Cherries	green state)
Coconut	Peas
Dates	Peppers
Figs	Pimientos
Guava	Pumpkin and squash
Peaches	Sweet corn
Pears	Sweet potatoes
Plums	Onion

The primary rule for safeguarding fruit to be dried is cleanliness. A hot, windy day with the sun shining is best for drying, but in areas where sunny days are rare, a small building with a stove and slatted shelves—called a dry house—is sometimes used.

The steps for drying fruit are elementary: gather, wash, slice or peel, sulphur for better color and to discourage souring, layer the fruits on trays, cover with a netting and let the sun go to work. When two-thirds dry (one or two days later), condition the fruit by holding it at room temperature for a week or two. Store in a dark, dry place.

Sun-dried fruits are generally flavorful when reconstituted with water, but time leaves its mark on sweet vegetation as readily as it does on sweet womenfolk. Shriveled, wrinkly, brittle and pallid, the prunes my friend and I found in a miner's shack abandoned in 1926 were like the bark of an ancient sycamore. Though those prunes still held the pit and heartmeat, they had seen better days.

Candying fruits, nuts, roots in sugar has been used in some households as a means of safekeeping goodies. Management of the heat is the prime skill in candying. Although I have candied foods, I cannot vouch for their keeping qualities because my houseful of nibblers nibble and I have lots of little neighborhood nibblers, too. While my young friends are visiting, I get a nibble of life, a glimpse into their sinless souls, and a beautiful, sweet nibble it is. Children give real reason for safekeeping the gifts of our earth.

Like sugar, honey is a natural preservative. Although my grandfather used to forage for honey trees and call on his brave friends to borrow the honey, the only bee tree my family found was fake and we learned about the mad, mad, mad, mad world of hornets. In addition to the rules about protecting yourself in the bee clinches and not destroying the hive when stealing sweets, the cardinal rule of honey-gathering is to leave some for the bees.

Safekeeping the earth's goods, preserving them for the future is an act of faith. Whether curing tidbits of meat, utilizing native herbs in drink, preserving with salt or sweets, canning or dehydration, living the natural life is man's pledge to be faithful to the earth.

Bibliography

MEATS

David, Elizabeth. *Spices, Salt and Aromatics in the English Kitchen.* Harmondsworth, Middlesex: Penguin Books Ltd., 1970.

Home Meat Curing. Chicago (110 North Wacker Drive): Morton Salt Company, 1969.

Processing Beef on the Farm. U.S. Dept. of Agriculture, Farmers' Bulletin 2209. Washington: G.P.O., 1965.

Processing Pork on the Farm. U.S. Dept. of Agriculture, Farmers' Bulletin 2138. Washington: G.P.O., 1967.

Protecting Home-cured Meat from Insects. U.S. Dept. of Agriculture, Home and Garden Bulletin 109. Washington: G.P.O., 1970.

NATIVE TEAS

Fernald, Merrit L.; Kinsey, A. C., and Rollins, Reed C. *Edible Wild Plants of Eastern North America,* revised edition. New York: Harper and Row, 1958.

Gibbons, Euell. *Stalking the Wild Asparagus.* New York: David McKay, 1962.

Leighton, Ann. *Early American Gardens.* Boston: Houghton Mifflin Company, 1970.

Porsild, A. E. "Edible Plants of the Arctic," *Arctic,* Vol. VI (March 1953).

FIZZY DRINKS

Bravery, H. E. *Home Brewing.* New York: Gramercy Publishers, 1965.

Terner, B. C. A.; Berry, C. J. J., and Marshall, A. I. *The Winemaker's Companion.* Don Mills, Canada: Mills and Boon, 1972.

PICKLES AND CANNING

Ball Blue Book, Home Canning. Muncie, Indiana: Ball Brothers Inc., 1956.

Home Canning. U.S. Dept. of Agriculture, Home and Garden Bulletin 8. Washington: G.P.O., 1965.

Making Pickles and Relishes at Home. U.S. Dept. of Agriculture, Home and Garden Bulletin 92. Washington, G.P.O., 1967.

CHEESES, POTTED MEATS AND BREAD

Cheese Varieties. U.S. Dept. of Agriculture, Agriculture Handbook 54. Washington: G.P.O., 1969.

Bibliography

David, Elizabeth. *French Provincial Cooking*. Harmondsworth, Middlesex: Penguin Books, Ltd., 1967.

Homemade Bread, Cake and Pastry. U.S. Dept. of Agriculture, Farmers' Bulletin 1775. Washington: G.P.O., 1942.

Making Cottage Cheese at Home. U.S. Dept. of Agriculture, Home and Garden Bulletin 129. Washington: G.P.O., 1967.

Montagné, Prosper. *Larousse Gastronomique*. New York: Crown Publishers, Inc., 1965.

Index

Alaska
  Eskimos of, 56–57
  Indians of, 60, 63
  "kink shrub" of, 66–67
  teas of, 69
Alcohol, curing meat and, 18–19
  See also Beer; Home-brewing;
    Wine
Alcohol content, 74
  hydrometer and, 75–76
Alder (*Alnus rubra*), 61
Aleut Indians, 63
American spikenard (*Aralia race-
  mosa*), 80, 81
Anthelmintic, 70
Apple blossom tea, 68
Apples
  canning of, 138
  drying of, 164
Applesauce, 138
Apricots
  candied, 167
  canned, 140
Asparagus, canning of, 128–29
Avens (*Geum urbanaum* and *G.*
  rivale), 61

Bacon curing, 26–30
Bacteria, 174
  canning and, 124–25, 126, 178
  cheese formation and, 107
  meat curing and, 18
Baker's yeast, 74
Balsam fir tea, 70
Basil tea, 175
Basswood, 67–68
Bean flours, baking bread with, 145
Beans
  canning, 134–35
  pickling, 176
Bearberry, 61–62

Beef
  corned, 32–36
  curing, 36–37
  dried, 36–37
  Kielbasa and, 53–54
  in pepperoni, 51
  potted, 122
  salami with, 50
  sausages with, 52–54
  sour beer marinade for, 84
  See also Meat
Beehives, gathering honey and,
  169–71, 181–82
Beer, home-brewed, 12, 176
  birch, 85–86
  cooking with sour, 84–85
  curing meat and, 19
  gill ale, 81–82
  ginger, 79
  Gorse, 82–83
  licorice, 85
  Mock Hops, 82
  molasses, 83–84
  sediment and, 85
  spruce, 77–78
  sugar in, 74–75
  See also Home-brewing
Beer Bread, 152
Bees, honey and, 170–71, 182
Beets, baby
  canning, 130, 131
  pickling, 176
Belle Curd cheese, 113–14
Bergamot (*Monarda didyma*), 63
Berries
  canning, 133–36
  pickling, 92
Berrywater, 77
Birch (*Betula lenta*), 63, 75
  tea, 58
  beer, 82, 85–86
Bitters, 83

Black spruce (*Picea mariana*), 63
Black walnuts, 158–59, 169
Blackberries
  canning, 135
  pickling, 104
Blossom teas, 58, 59, 67–68
Blue Mountain tea, 13, 65
Blueberries, canning, 136
Boneset, 63–64
Borage (*Borago officinalis*), 64
Botulinum clostridium, canning
  and, 124–25, 178
Brandied strawberries, 129
Bratwurst, 49
Bread baking, 14, 144–53, 175–79
  Beer, 152
  cheese, 149
  with cracked grains, 152
  flours for, 144–45, 152, 179
  with fruit, 148–49
  Italian, 153
  methods of, 147–48
  molasses wheat, 152
  peanut butter, 149
  pizza dough, 150
  potato, 151
  rolls, 148, 149–50
  Sausage, 53
  sourdough, 145–47
  Sweet Potato, 151
Brewer's yeast, 74
Brewing, *see* Home-brewing
Briar tea, 69
Brine
  butter in, 154–55
  curing meats and, 19
  types of pickling, 91, 176–77
  See also Pickling and brining
Bubbling off, 76–77
Burdock root (*Arctium lappa*) tea,
  64
Butter, 153–57, 179
  butternut, 156, 179
  goose, 155
  peanut, 155–56
Buttermilk, 154
Butternut butter, 156
Butternut oil, 157–58

Camembert cheese, 107, 112
Candying, 167–69, 181

Canning, 13–14, 124–43, 177–78
  applesauce, 138
  asparagus, 128–29
  beets, 131
  corn, 136
  fish, 136–37
  fruits, 132–36, 138–40, 142
  greens, 126–27
  methods of, 125
  peas, 131–32
  rhubarb, 128
  squash, 130–31
  strawberries, 129
  tomatoes, 140–41
  utensils for, 125–26, 178
Cantaloupe, canned, 137
Carbon dioxide, home-brewing and,
  74
Caribou
  curing, 39
  in sausage, 50
Carrot kraut, 91–92
Carrots, canning, 142
Casings, sausage, 21, 43–44
Casserole, squash, 130–31
Cassina, 65–66
Catsup, making, 13, 103
  with hickory nuts, 161
Cauliflower, pickled, 176
Celery, canning, 142
Chamomile tea (*Anthemis nobilis*),
  64, 175
Cheddar cheese, 108, 114
Cheese bread, 149
Cheese dumplings, 110
Cheese potting, 13, 107–17, 177
  Belle Curd, 113–14
  classification of, 107–8
  farmer, 109–10
  formation of, 107
  Fromage Bleu, 112–13
  Kochkase, 111–12
  Schmierkase, 109–10
  spices in, 114
Cherry Bounce, 86–87
Cherries
  candied, 167–68
  canned, 134
  in pie, 134
Chicken
  hickory stuffing for, 161

potted, 118–19
Chickweed (*Stellaria media*) tea, 64
Chinese teas, 57
Chutney, Anne's Pickled, 104
Cinnamon rolls, 149–50
Cinquefoil, "kink shrub," 66–67
Comfrey tea, 64
Corn
  canning of, 136
  pickling of, 92, 176
Corned beef, 32–36, 174
Corned Rump, 35
Cottage cheese, 107
Country Pizza, 30–31
Cranberries, canning, 142
Cream cheese, 71, 107
Creeping Charley (*Nepeta gle-choma*), 66
Cucumber pickles, 95–99, 176
  brining of, 95–96
  "Counterfeit," 104
  dill, 98–99
  sour, 97
  sweet, 97–98
  "Swifty Chunks," 99
Cucumbers in vinegar, 104
Culpeper, Virginia, 63–64, 130
Curd, cheese making and, 107–8
Curing meat, 10–12, 18–40, 174–75
  beef, 32–37
  equipment for, 20–22
  game meat, 39–40
  lamb, 38
  pork, 26–32, 174
  sausage, 18, 20–22, 174
  smokehouse for, 21–22
  See also specific meats
Currant Crush, 86, 87
Currants, canning, 138

Dandelions
  Gorse from, 82–83
  pickled, 176
Darwin, Erasmus, 57
Decanting of home-brew, 85
Digestion and teas, 63, 70
Dill, 90–91
Dill pickles, 98–99
Dock root, 59, 64–65, 70
Drying beef, 36–37

Drying fruits, 162–63, 164–67, 180–181
  oven and, 166–67
  sulphuring and, 164–65
  vacuum packing and, 166
Drying tea herbs, 58–60

Eggs, potted, 117
Elder tea, 58, 65
Elderberries, canning, 139
English walnuts, fried, 162
Evergreen perennial, 60
Eyebright (*Euphrasia americana*), 65

False dragon head (*Phystogia virginiana*), 66
Farmer cheese, 109–10
Fennel seed tea (*Foeniculum vulgare*), 65, 175
Fermentation lock, home-brewing and, 76–77
Fern roots, pickled, 92–93
Figs, canned, 140
Fish
  canning, 136–37
  potting, 117
Flour, baking bread and, 144–45, 152, 179
Flower blossom tea, 59
Fruit
  in bread, 148–49
  candied, 167–68, 181
  canning, 132–36
  drying, 162–67, 180–81
  fermentation of, 76–77
  pickled, 104
Fudge, honey, 169

Game meat
  curing, 39–40
  sausages of, 49–50
Garlic Sausage, 47
German Pork Chops, 133–34
Gill ale, 81–82
Gill-over-the-ground (*Glecoma hederacea*), 81
Ginger beer, 79
Ginger tea, 75, 175
Gluten, bread baking and, 145, 179

Goldenrod (*Solidago odora*) tea, 65, 175
Gooseberries, canning, 138–39
Goosebutter, 155
Gorse, home-brewing, 82–83
Grapes, canning, 140
Green beans, canning, 134–35
Green Scrapple, 127
Green tomatoes, 141–42
  pickling, 176
Greens
  canning, 126–27
  pickling, 176
Ground ivy tea, 81, 175
Gruyère cheese, 107

Halman, Frank, 57, 58–59, 70
Ham
  cooked in hay, 32
  lamb, 38–39
  stuffed, 31–32
Ham curing, 26–30
  dry, 28, 29
  sugar, 28
  pickled, 28–29
Heal-all (*Collinsonia canadensis*), 66
Hemlock tea, 70
Herb teas, 12–13, 56–72, 173
  effects of, 57
  identification of, 60
  preparing, 58–60
  types of, 61–72, 175–76
Herb vinegar, 101–3
Hickory nuts, 160–62, 179
  fried, 162
  with fudge, 169
  squirrels and, 162
Hickory Stuffing, 161
Hog jowl, 31
Holly (*Ilex vomitoria*), 65–66
Holsteiner sausage, 52–53
Holy Herb, 61
Home-brewing, 12, 73–88, 176
  gill ale, 81–82
  ginger beer, 79
  Gorse, 82–83
  "Mock Hops," 82
  molasses beer, 83–84
  process of, 74–75
  sarsaparilla, 80–81

spruce beer, 77–78
storage for, 87–88
utensils for, 75–76
of wine, 74–76, 176
Home Sausage, 45–46
Honey
  gathering, 170–72, 181–82
  preserving with, 169, 181
Honey Fudge, 169
Honeysuckle blossom tea, 68
Hop flowers (*Humulus lupulus*), 66, 83, 85
Horehound (*Marrubium*), 66
Horse balm (*Collinsonia canadenis*), 66
Horseradish sauce, potted pork and, 121
Huckleberries
  canning, 136
  pudding, 136
Hydrometer, home-brewing and, 75–76

Immersion heater, home-brewing and, 75
Indians
  of Alaska, 56–57, 60, 61–62
  pickling by, 92–93
  seeds and, 163
  teas of, 69
Insecticides, 68
Italian bread, 153
Italian Pork Sausage, 47–48
Italian salami, 50–51

Jars, canning, 125–26, 131, 178
Jelly, mulberry, 133–34
Jerky, 36–37
Joepye, 63–64

Kielbasa sausage, 53–54
"Kink shrub," 66–67
Kinnikinik, 61–62
Knackwurst sausage, 54
Knotgrass (*Polygonum*) tea, 67
Kochkase cheese, 111–12

Labrador tea, 13, 56, 67, 175
Lactic acids
  cheese and, 107
  pickling and, 90

Lamb, 37
  curing, 38
  ham, 38–39
Leaching of pickles, 97
Leaves, teas of, 58–59
Lemonade, Lively, 86
Licorice beer, 82, 85
Licorice root tea, 175
Lima beans, canning, 142
Limburger cheese, 107, 114–15
Linden tea (*Tilia americana*), 13, 67–68, 175
Lively Lemonade, 86
Livestock
  buying, 24–25
  raising, 15–17
Log perch, canning, 137

Mad-dog skullcap (*Scutellaria lateriflora*), 66
Malt beer, 74–75
Marinade, sour beer, 84–85
Marjoram tea, 175
"May tea," 68
Mayweed (*Anthemis cotula*), 64
Meats
  curing, 10–12, 18–40, 174–75
  dried, 36–37
  potted, 106, 118–22, 174–75
  sour beer marinade for, 84–85
  See also specific meats
Medicinal teas, 57, 63, 64, 71
Mettwurst sausage, 54
Milk, cheese and, 107–8
Mint family, 13, 66
"Mock Hops," 82
Molasses beer, 82–84
Molasses wheat bread, 152
Moose meat
  curing, 10, 11, 40
  sausage, 50
Motherwort (*Leonurus cardiaca*), 68
Mugwort (*Artemisia vulgaris*), 68
Mulberries
  canning, 133
  jelly, 133–34
Mushrooms, pickled, 105

Nectarines, canned, 140

Nettle (*Urtica dioica*) tea, 68–69, 175
New Jersey tea (*Ceanothus Americanus*), 58, 69
Northern bearberries, 62–63
Nut bread, 149
Nut brittle, 168–69
Nut butters, 155–57, 179
Nut trees, 162, 180
Nuts, 157–62, 179–80
  spiced, 160
  sugared, 168–69, 181

Oatmeal bread, 152
Oil of spruce, 75
Olive oil, homemade, 94–95
Olives, brined, 94–95
Onions, canning, 130, 132
Oswego tea, 63, 175

Peaches
  candied, 168
  canning, 139
Peanut brittle, 168–69
Peanut butter, homemade, 155–56
Peanut butter bread, 149
Pears
  canning, 142
  drying, 164
Peas, green
  canning, 130, 131–32
  soup, 132
Pepperoni, 51–52
  with homemade pizza, 52
Pennyroyal (*Hedeoma pulegioides*), 66
Peppermint, 66
Peppers, pickled, 100–1, 176
Perch, canned, 137
Persimmon (*Diospyros virginia*), 69
  beer, 12
  canning, 142
  tea, 13, 58, 175
Pickling and brining, 13, 89–105, 173, 174, 176–77
  brine for, 91, 176–77
  of carrots, 91–92
  chutney, 104
  cucumbers, 95–99, 176
  fruits, 104

Pickling and brining (cont.)
left-over vegetables, 99–100
mushrooms, 105
olives, 94–95
peppers, 100–1
utensils for, 90
See also specific vegetables
Pie
cherry, 134
Pork Tamale, 46–47
rhubarb, 128
Pigs
buying, 24–26
slaughtering, 42
Pine tea, 70
Pizza
Country, 30–31
dough for, 150
with pepperoni, 52
Plantain (*Plantago*), 69
Plants, teas from, 58–60
Plum blossom tea, 68
Plums, canning, 139–40
Polish Sausage, 53–54
Poplar leaf tea (*Populus tremulo-ides*), 69
Pork
curing, 26–32
potted, 120–22
smoked, 29–30
Pork chops, German, 133–34
Pork liver, potted, 121–22
Pork roast, fresh, 84
Pork sausage, 42–55
Bratwurst, 49
drying, 45
Garlic, 47
Holsteiner, 52–53
Italian, 47–48
Kielbasa, 53–54
Knackwurst, 54
Plain, 48–49
stuffing casing of, 43–45
Summer, 45–46
Tamale Pie, 46–47
Pork Summer Sausage, 45–46
Pork tongue, potted, 121
Port Salut cheese, 107
Potato Bread, 151
Potted foods, 13, 106–123, 174–75
beef, 122

cheeses, 107–117, 177
chicken, 118–19
eggs, 117
fish, 117
meats, 106, 118–22, 174–75
pork, 120–22
utensils for, 108
Preserving, 173–82
Pumpkin seeds
drying, 163, 180
tea of, 69

Radish Top Soup, 127
Raspberries, canning, 134
Red root, 69
Rennet, cheese and, 108
Rheumatism root, 60
Rhubarb, 128
River rat sausage, 50
Roots
tea from, 59–60, 175
identification of, 60
Roquefort cheese, 107, 112–13
Rolls, 148–50
Rose blossom tea, 68
Rosehip tea, 69, 175
Rye flour, 145, 179

Sage (*Salvia officinalis*), 69–70
St. John's plant (*Artemisia vulgaris*), 68
Salad, scurvy grass in, 70
Salami, 50–51
Salt
curing meat and, 18, 174
pickling and, 90–91
Saltpeter, curing meat and, 18, 174
Sarsaparilla
brewing, 12, 80–81
root tea from, 175
Sassafras, 70–75
Sassafras root, elixir of, 77, 80, 175
in sarsaparilla, 80–81
Sauce
horseradish, 121
rhubarb, 128
Sauerkraut, 90–91, 176
Sausage, 41–55
Bratwurst, 49
casings for, 21, 43–44
curing, 18, 20–22, 174

drying, 45
of game meat, 49–50
Garlic, 47
green tomatoes and, 141–42
Holsteiner, 52–53
Home, 45–46
Italian, 47–48
Kielbasa, 53–54
Plain, 48–49
Tamale Pie, 46–47
Sausage Bread, 53
Savory tea, 175
Scurvy grass (*Cochlearia officin-alis*), 70
Sediment, home-brewing and, 85
Seeds
drying, 163–64, 180
teas from, 59
Semisoft cheeses, 107
Seneca Indians, 92
Sherbet, strawberry, 130
Simpler's Joy (*Verbena officinalis*), 71
Skullcap, mad-dog, 66
Slaughterhouse, 24, 26
Slippery elm tea, 175
Smokehouse, 21–22
Smoking meats, 18, 19
pork, 29–30
Snakeroot tea, 175
"Soda pop," homemade, 86
Soft drinks, 74–75
Sorrel (*Rumex acetosa*), 70
Soup
green pea, 132
peanut butter, 156
Radish Top, 127
Sour beer, cooking with, 184–85
Sour pickles, 97
Sourdough, 145–47
Soybean bread, 152
Soybean butter, 157
Soybean flour, 145, 152, 157
Spanish peanuts, 168
Spearmint, 66
Spicebush (*Lindera benzoin*), 70
Spiced Nuts, 160
Spices, pickling and, 90–91
Spinach, pickled, 176
Spruce beer, 77–78
Spruce tea, 70

Squash
canning, 130
casserole of, 130–31
seeds of, 163, 180
Sticky buns, 148–50
Stinging nettle, 68–69
Strawberries
brandied, 129
canning, 129–30
sherbet, 130
Sugar
curing meat and, 18, 28, 30
home-brewing and, 74–76
Sulphuring fruit, 164–65, 180
Sumach (*Rhus glabra*), 70–71
Sun-dried fruit, 165–66, 180–81
Sunflower seeds, 163–64, 180
Swamp alder bark tea, 61
Sweet birch tea, 63, 175
Sweet goldenrod, 65
Sweet pickles, 97–98
Sweet Potato bread, 151
Sweet Potato and Walnut Cro-quettes, 159
Sweet rolls, 148–50
"Swifty Chunks," 99
Swiss chard, pickled, 176
Swiss cheese, 107
Syrup, canning fruit and, 132–33

Tamale Pie, Pork, 46–47
Teas, native, 12–13, 56–72, 173
effects of, 57
processing herbs for, 58–60
types of, 61–72, 175–76
Thistle (*Cirsium palustre*), 71
Thoroughwort, 63–64
Thyme tea, 71–72, 175
Tomatoes
canning, 140–41
green, 141–42, 176
pickled, 101, 176
Soft, 35
Tongue, corned, 35–36
Trichinae, 43, 174
Trichinosis, 21, 174

Vegetables
potted, 106–7
in vinegar, 104
See also Pickling and brining

Index

Venison, 11
  sausage of, 49
Verbena tea, 71, 175
Vervain tea, 71, 175
Vinegar
  curing meat and, 18, 19
  homemade, 101
  medicinal uses of, 102–3
  pickling with, 90, 97
  as purifier, 101
  vegetables in, 104
Violet (*Viola odorata*) tea, 71

Walnut Roast, 159
Walnut and Sweet Potato Croquettes, 159
Walnuts, 157, 179
  black, 158–59, 169
  English, 162
  sugared, 159
Wheat, baking bread with, 144–45,
  179

Whey, cheese and, 107
Wild allspice tea, 70
Wild marjoram (*Origanum vul-
  gare*) tea, 71–72, 175
Wild sarsaparilla tea, 80
Wild snowball, 69
Wild Thyme (*Thymus serpyllum*)
  tea, 71–72, 175
Wine, home-brewing of, 74–76, 176
  sugar in, 74–75
Wintergreen extract, 85–86
Witch-hazel, 72
Witches herb (*Artemisia vulgaris*),
  68
Wormwood tea, 83

Yaupon tea, 65–66
Yeast, 145
  home-brewing and, 74–76

Zucchini squash, canning, 130